W9-BUR-986

Praise for *Look at This Blue*

"Here is a lifetime, relentless, inviting us bravely to sit in a circle facing the fire, speaking. Allison's new collection covers her poetic depth and practice: travels, research, vision and visions, her wide wingspan—saving the people, the planet, and creatures. It is timely as all her books have been through the decades. Yet, the approach is radical, experimental. She meditates and dances through the trails of the text. Love and suffering, document and lyrical flight, human core and cosmic interrelationship, woman's body and explosive mind. A prizewinner all the way. A warm, true heart."

—Juan Felipe Herrera

"Song from both above and within a texture of bad change, imbued with beauty, being in and of nature. This language, these careful lines, implicates us all as bits of process of extinction, violent—humans, together with the Xerces blue butterfly and California's so many other spectacular species, lovingly named. Voices, vegetation, animals, human recall and event, like scratchings or petroglyphs. Who's speaking? The record. A gorgeous, scary poem."

—Alice Notley

"Both ode and elegy for our natural and man-made environments, Allison Hedge Coke's *Look at This Blue* speaks of California's inevitable loss, its 'temporal melt,' its 'death-wish façade.' Hedge Coke calligraphies this tragedy and mythos with such poignance that you will be riveted until the collection's very last line. *Look at This Blue* is not only timely; it is necessary."

—Lynne Thompson

"How blue are you? Xerces-butterfly blue, coyote-eye blue, lake blue, Mission blue: this is the blue of beauty and the blue of grief. *Look at This Blue* is a necessary reckoning with the ongoing, disastrous, criminal genocide perpetuated in the Golden State, amongst the beauty and riches of its landscape. As Hedge Coke writes, the poem is 'the offering we make.'"

—Eleni Sikelianos

"Allison Adelle Hedge Coke sings California with a garden of images, all life, named and splendidly watered by bewitching words—but this is no romantic paean. She documents genocide, massacres, slavery, arsons, lies, the laments of the pushed out and knocked down. Here's the hardest truth, wrapped in lyric." **—Luis J. Rodríguez**

"Allison Adelle Hedge Coke's *Look at This Blue* is a song for California: a poem as big, as diverse, as ambitious as the state it celebrates. Or do I mean the state it eulogizes? Or do I mean the state whose histories it sets straight? Or do I mean the state this poem seeks to save? Or do I mean the state of the poet whose story is part and parcel of the story of this same state in all its grim and glorious broken beauty? Yes, I mean these things and more. Much more. This is a poem whose borders extend beyond geography and territory and history. This is a poem to be lived."

—Dean Rader

"Allison Adelle Hedge Coke is one of the most important and innovative environmental writers of our time. *Look at This Blue* urgently asks us to see the wondrous biodiversity of the planet amidst the violent ravages of colonialism, capitalism, and ecological imperialism. Throughout, this cyclical poem sows dreams of a 'bettering world' where our relationships with the earth and more-than-human species are replenished through justice, protection, and love." **—Craig Santos Perez**

"From Ishi to Riverside fairy shrimp, from sandhill cranes to vast human damage, Allison Adelle Hedge Coke calls out and calls to California in *Look at This Blue*. The book is a poem is a list, naming the eighty-four who died in the Camp Fire in Paradise, the millions killed in their native landscapes and internment camps and everywhere else. It reminds us of the extinct Xerces blue butterfly and, page after page, of the endangered ones: delta smelt, riparian woodrat, Sierra Nevada yellow-legged frog, Mono Lake diving beetle, finback whale, a list that, as it grows, becomes profound, tragic, gorgeous, overwhelming, and eventually a song. But a song not to be sung without the accompanying verses of greed and power, of politics, massacre, incarceration, exclusion. Not even the missing are missing: we are all included. The title repeats through the text as a chorus, a tow-line to hang on to, at one point referring to the chance mutation of coyote eye color, at another, the Hidden Lake bluecurl flower, fifty of which will fit on a penny. This is a book for the world we currently inhabit, the long unstoppable chaos, the season of losing everything we love. Listen. Let yourself belong. 'Recite their names now,' Hedge Coke asks us, coaxes us, dares us in her clear voice, unafraid.

And then she names an appendix of resource links: 'do the work.'"

—Molly Fisk

"Holding this book in your hand, you catch the scent of high desert salvia and a whiff of charred ancient forests. Pyrocumulus loom over this text, an assemblage in the vein of Juan Felipe Herrera and C. D. Wright, etched in chants of forewarning and loss. Hedge Coke's reckoning with the genocide of the Indigenous and the mass extinction of endemic species bares the roots of conflagration throughout 'Indian Country, California, every bit.' *Look at This Blue* is itself a blue flame that comes to us in time."

—Sesshu Foster

"*Look at This Blue* is a fiercely pulsating journey of love and despair. The earth crackles, the body heaves in these wrenching snapshots of personal, historical, and environmental disasters. You want to look away, but you can't, as Allison Hedge Coke chronicles all the ways we are broken, our bone-deep griefs. Above and beneath these losses, she offers us singular joys: the trill of sandhill cranes, a girl with 'eyes the green of August,' small porpoises that 'undulate in air.' A list of resources at the end urges us toward the work of survival. We are still on the hook." **—Diana García**

"In *Look at This Blue*, Allison Hedge Coke pulls us into a meditation on the entangled history of California's ecological and racial catastrophes, which shape the place's past and present. In an unapologetic disquisition focused on the actualities of California's Indigenous peoples and their land, Hedge Coke lays bare the course that made way to the burning, flooding, splintering realities that shape California today. Both astonishing and piercing, hopeful and solemn, *Look at This Blue* plunges the reader into the fractal distortion of seeing the sun from underneath the water. This is a poem of urgency, of sorrow and memory, a call for us to see anew and change the destructive path we're on before we are all consumed by it."

—Matthew Shenoda

"What Hedge Coke provides readers in the pages that follow is the lightning rod. Her long poem slips in and out of images of violence against the land, specifically California, the flora and fauna and many immigrants and Indigenous peoples of that land, the poor and cast out and overlooked and neglected and abused of that land, ever aware of the undercurrents that connect each transgression. While I've grown suspicious that one can give voice to the voiceless without doing further violence, these lines are not acts of ventriloquism, nor even quiet moments of witnessing. These are the aftershocks of the violences we as a nation would not see, haunting the periphery until there is nowhere we can look without being made at last to see. But in this litany of those who have been lost and those who are at risk, so too there is an act of preservation, a summons, and offering. If not promise, then a charge, a spark, to move us along. This book is like nothing I've seen from Hedge Coke before. It was just what I needed to read right now."

—Abigail Chabitnoy, *Orion Magazine*

LOOK AT THIS BLUE

Also by Allison Adelle Hedge Coke

Dog Road Woman

Off-Season City Pipe

Streaming

Blood Run

Burn

The Year of the Rat

Rock, Ghost, Willow, Deer

LOOK AT THIS BLUE

A Poem

Allison Adelle Hedge Coke

COFFEE HOUSE PRESS
Minneapolis
2022

Copyright © 2022 by Allison Adelle Hedge Coke
Cover image © Logan Bush/Shutterstock.com
Cover design by Carlos Esparza
Book design by Bookmobile
Author photograph © Adrianne Mathiowetz

Coffee House Press books are available to the trade through our primary distributor, Consortium Book Sales & Distribution, cbsd.com or (800) 283-3572. For personal orders, catalogs, or other information, write to info@coffeehousepress.org.

Coffee House Press is a nonprofit literary publishing house. Support from private foundations, corporate giving programs, government programs, and generous individuals helps make the publication of our books possible. We gratefully acknowledge their support in detail in the back of this book.

Excerpts have been previously published in *Cordite*, *Walt's Corner/Long Islander News*, *AWP Writers Chronicle*, *Ploughshares*, an anthology for *Playa*, and a *Poetry & Science* group poet chapbook by Scarlet Tanager Books.

LIBRARY OF CONGRESS CATALOGING-IN-PUBLICATION DATA

Names: Hedge Coke, Allison Adelle, author.
Title: Look at this blue : a poem / Allison Adelle Hedge Coke.
Identifiers: LCCN 2021053386 (print) | LCCN 2021053387 (ebook) | ISBN 9781566896207 (paperback) | ISBN 9781566896290 (epub)
Subjects: LCGFT: Poetry.
Classification: LCC PS3553.O4366 L66 2022 (print) | LCC PS3553.O4366 (ebook) | DDC 811/.54—dc23/eng/20211029
LC record available at https://lccn.loc.gov/2021053386
LC ebook record available at https://lccn.loc.gov/2021053387

PRINTED IN THE UNITED STATES OF AMERICA

29 28 27 26 25 24 23 22 1 2 3 4 5 6 7 8

Look at This Blue

for my blue butterfly, Hazel Brianne

for Marija, Diana & Paul,
for the quiet rooms

for California, our beloved

once, the world was gleaming, open, we entered
unknowing, believing all we came to
we must deserve, knowing we did not faced
extinction

"The path we have taken has rotted
Ignite, stand upright, conduct yourself like lightning"

—Tanya Tagaq, "Retribution"

an assemblage

LOOK AT THIS BLUE

Look at This Blue

Xerces blue butterfly *from the sand dunes of San Francisco*
first-known American butterfly to become extinct due to humans
first known

Redwood burls cut like blisters shaved from trunks
poach life source from root
killing giants in knobby growth removals
baseline / canopy-height bud tissue
unsprouted genetic code for clone of parent-tree emergence—

Barrel at my mouth, ready-cocked held there
by my baby brother's bared grip.

Lemon-wedge half-moon pops over
flat Cosumnes shallows
over sweet sound, low rustle in Lodi water
chortle trill night language from standing
cranes, sandhills, they've been there
all along, standing still knee-deep in station pools.

Orion hovering eastward drawn, readied.
Someone slinks past doorjamb
each choke hold felled vaporizes cognizance.

In a world fast shaking herself loose
from diabolical torrent.

Rising throttle song above throttled breath
choked out between calligraphies,
madness clenched fury unfurled release
misery met in each pummeled break
it's not over.

Sleep in despair sleeping moth-tongue, unrolled against central incisors,
human-throated, deep yearns for saxophone
trachea windpipe—
Sandhills chortle only saving grace wetlands marshalled.
Nothing here on guardian watch.

Riverside.
Reaching back for slipped skateboard
he was hit so hard he flew while breaking.

A crow above, whose wings were sunning, swooped
at the same time the car careened to halt
on Martin Luther King Road

near Bordwell Park, Eastside, where the speed limit suddenly increases while approaching two close crosswalks leading to homes from Stratton Community Center, Bordwell, Emerson Elementary—Eastside; Black, brown kids; elders—
Anyone can see someone once worked this out.

Ishi died thirteen years before I was born,

so I have no nice anecdotes about knowing him when I was a child. I'm sorry.

—Ursula K. Le Guin

It was custom to be introduced by name, not to utter own. UC Berkeley chose man/Ishi for a name for him, which he (accepted).

He worked as a research assistant in the anthropology department.
He was placed into a museum in the anthropology department.

Yana continued living in California.

After declaration that Ishi
was the last of his people, at least
four other Yahi were seen in the
bush.

Yana [was] an agglutinative, polysynthetic
language with SVO word order. The Yana
language was distinctive in having different
word forms used by male and female speakers,
an unusual trait that does not exist in the other
languages of this region.

1999, Ishi's brain returned to Yana people, his closest relatives

"It's all going to burn," says man accused of setting Holy Fire

First the puma in Santa Paula palm branch, then coyotes, fox, rabbits
appear, birds overcome sky plume,
then the entire yard a carpet of undulating fleas
so thick wrapping that bread bags over feet and ankles
barely made it passable.
Everything escaping heat from fire-stormed arson 120,000 acres
blanket-fired Los Padres National Forest and more

choking like the child they found, still hung—

Sleep in the dream of bettering world.
Sleep in the dream/nightmare woken.

What we carry howls boggling
her cheek contorts in flame unfanned yet fanning.

She eclipses all asunder, all broken.
Scar face vision in temporal melt.

Somewhere on my left face, you can still see
where it was sewn back on.

On the right, the line across eyelid
where it was sewn back on.
On the abdomen the line
where it was sewn back, sewn back, sewn back.
Somewhere on my right hand
where it was sewn.

All the heres and theres
where sewn.

All the labia biopsies, removals, explorations, assaults, sewn.

1985–2000. 1963–1996.

What we carry weeps wet-haired
her cheek contorts when sprayed by guard.

From the first time she attempted, her neck ached.

Meanwhile, here, a third body in Baldwin Hills fire, more missing
arson again
someone *is out there.*

Look at This Blue

Palos Verdes blue from the Palos Verdes Peninsula
one of the best claims to being world's rarest butterfly
first thought extinct by development
rediscovered by Rick Rogers, Rudi Mattoni, and Timothy Dahlum
at the Defense Fuel Support Point in San Pedro

newly returned lays eggs on deerweed
notice the patterning on the underside of wing

Child choked out, belt at throat.
She returned to me in dreams.
Child choked out, belt at throat.
She returned to me in dreams.
Child choked out, belt at throat.
She returned to me in dreams.
Child choked out, belt at throat.
She returned to me in dreams.
Child choked out, belt at throat.
She returned to me in dreams.
Child choked out, belt at throat.
She returned to me in dreams.
Child choked out, belt at throat.
She returned to me in dreams.
Child choked out, belt at throat.
She returned to me in dreams.

They were only there seeking psychiatric help.

She'd been exceptionally mean for days

Their grandson rode along while they sorted what they could of it, while her

schizophrenia played out all sorts.

They turned into the intersection by the mall in Ventura
a big tank of a thing T-boned them
right down the middle of the car.
So concussed, cops gave their ATM PIN to taxi home.

He'd lost a tooth. Grandson's nose broken.
She broke a leg. All three concussed.
The dog in the other car was dizzy, some say.

Later, she took a call from her son, headed out to wire away her war widow's pension.

Walking on an unattended broken leg. Senior living.

Remember, along the way, the murdered sow bear, her cubs taken for claws.

We're all just symptoms of something massive faster over
they're killing us.
weaponizing nature, sanctifying arms, consecrating each trigger-flexed hand.

Dad, in his eighties, on the trailer roof sprayer in hand fighting back ignition
not leaving until everyone leaves,
or the time he battled out of being rolled, just smoothly
turned his cane horizontal,
asking punks who should join him when he dies, soon enough,
until they scramble
cross K-Mart parking lot.

Trigger turned to face, every right to bear bitter, every night-schemed
daybreak flash
no need to fictionalize this dude
is what he is, what man made, what man.

Sliced labia squamous, first
somewhere midtwenties.

Missing children, women, taken
somewhere.
For me it was a gulley, a pond, a base, a van, a hall, a window—

Here, where her hair shone blue-black all over her time.
Where, throughout our childhood, we never cherished it.
Yet when found on others, we loved them, coveted
long, horselike tails our lovers threw over their
shoulders, our own blue-black love we needed to know, never felt,
until the later years when we couldn't get enough of her.

What was wronged there, woven?
What bind was pulled when dog stole soup?

Blankets, Pendletons, all blue as well, some with black
some with red, yellow to bring sun
into this longing place, this place of loss, longing.

Throughout childhood, we never cherished it.
In her pyre, we gathered all of these with her, let it smolder loved.

INS showed up morning sometime
after he demanded IRS pay him back-owed arrears.
"When were you last in Mexico?" they asked his wife.
Our honeymoon, 1950. "When will you return to
Mexico?"

they
ask.

We're too old to travel, they note.

His call came late. Where are your mother's

naturalization papers? Her green card. Can you fax them
to INS, to IRS? They put your mother in a van to deport

to Mexico. She's Canadian, you note. Black hair, black eyes,
short, dark complexioned, Mexican enough, he says.

SB-622 Civil Detention Facilities: State Investigation.
Within 90 days after the individual's death,

the Department of Justice shall make a public report
Could be any mama.

Once a flat

flat

shell

brain husk
with no dendrite,
no axon, no crystalline mass
branch impulse at synapse
no hope within husks of men, self-molded
set to burgeon, fixate boulders,
once marbled giant, now fixed flat
to hurl, catapult incendiary, tension-
launching slingshot (de)vice *Tweet*

Let it be an arms race,
we will outmatch them
at every pass and outlast
them all. Any them,
at all.

Then it was
done, or almost so.

State mirrors cried:

beautiful boy,
made to eat cat feces,
vomit, pepper sprayed, made
to live in a cabinet, box,
bound and gagged at eight because you might be gay.

Beautiful child taken at ten, beaten, tortured,
Malnourished; whose mother, father
tore into, pummeled for coming out,
for coming out.

California's largest utility could face murder charges . . .

if found responsible for sparking recent, deadly wildfires

around the state

Daily Caller

PG&E pleads guilty to 84 counts of involuntary manslaughter over Camp fire

LA Times

Equations made to name propensities, longing, departures,
intrusion, infusions, all as one needs
to be viable in the state or lack thereof.

Where man goes, comes inevitable loss, it was
always this way, intrusion, infusions, all as one needs.

After tens of thousands of generations, now
lain a mile or so deep under grounds long overwashed
in a world gone awry, the
remains of the day buried by the flow and ebb to it.
This morning 185 mph winds wind.

Where fish caches still lie, untouched and
frozen beneath our own remains, introspective delights,
egomanias, here they lie
awaiting rebirths into sparks of life above
even still untouched, cold there. Waiting
for fires to bear life, carbons still, like embers, cold yet.

Here, we once knew balance, achieved it, lived it.
Any one of them left to themselves if they
maneuvered away
from agreement reached with all of the natural world.
Where only one of the many
now overthrown and imbalanced
by intrusion by who left ideology of
balance for warscapes, resourcing, in a way
tangled to harness everything met.

In some discovery mode and taking, it never
ended, still goes on and now
even rainwater for sale so harnessed
for commodity, for resource in a green
time now long-over, browned in drought made
by sourcing rain givers, savanna grasses,
forests, sea oats in a time where everything is
commodified, so taken
to other places now without, in this time
of no ways to meander in a
continual manner, now, everything must
shift, we will surely not endure, stones sigh.

There is not joy in it and man is now the antibiosis
symbiotic relation
shared with all completely unearthed
scathed, hotter, only those
who see past retain understanding
time, place, safety give back
to keep balance sure, a timely whole
equal, many trees
canopy, rain,
give life again to the spark of energy necessary
to star starwood reborn again
lifting lights on deserts over
geological spots giving spherical visitations.

We need balance. Need keep from
what may kill us all what may
end us. Distinguish an atom, a
gathered molecule, something we must
in each and every touch in this life in
every single moment of solitude and in
silence in the coming and going of River and her
embodiment of so many other beings she
nurtures to replenish us with the life givers the
fish she bears and birds who seek her
for snails and protection as we seek River for
healing to rekindle us in our own winterings.
Now is the time to return to what we do with
our partnerships in life, the cranes impressing
us for generation upon generation giving us
dances and life and reason and approach to
enjoy the reason we were gifted these particular atoms.

To stone walls, to everything residual here
languages morph
balance standing on one leg and the other,
jet forward leap, crane dance
all balance and reason understood every motive
or deference, rearing young
conditioning note, absolute calling for more
rain all around in beauty bringing
snail to surface keeping predator under cover
searching for mouse rather than bird prey.

Shell-shocked. Gullied.

After he cut this hand, severed tendon,
punched this face, mocked,
bruised, cut—punched again—
his Ventura County public defender, a woman,
asked me to drop charges so he
wouldn't miss class.
Not happening.
Not happening.
Not happening.
Guilty; she won Suspended Imp anyway.
This is how roadside trash pick-up equates even.

Broken branch in canopy, trees, like fingers, like stiff blade through my right hand,

bone handle separating knuckles

like gales tearing muscle bearing my keen weight.

Or E. coli.

Some salad in the back aisle,

invader, like this guy.

Too idiotic to merit note, past criminal code

when pressing limits, cruelties

as method of stopping poems so

they could not escape

no matter the muse-scape. Santa Anas, floods, frost on orange grove—

All that counted elsewise,

was any snowfall on Topatopa

something lost on death-wish facade

calling itself *man*.

Ghost knocks pounded behind my head on the wall

when he tried to stay here.

Enigma, can we still use this?
Maybe we are, I am.
Not in the way Lopez would
call *Bruja* when plant hangers split,
oranges flew, unaided.
Chairs bobbed like mergansers in quakes.
Northridge, maybe wildest
we'd met. Pipe bomb, some believed.
In the still no one questioned
some thrilled by variance, by her shaking us loose.

Behind us Limoneira, a town of a camp
now some suburbia development,
then all sorts of workers, growers, since 1893,
Rancho Sespe, Flores y Cantos, la Lucha we would go—
Santa Paula, Fillmore, Piru
Oxnard strawberries, Saticoy records, Ventura gold beaches
hot peppers shouldering Blood Alley Ventura Freeway, 126
oleanders, eucalyptus, rhododendron.
I came from the camps. Not these, but I served these
children. Decades ago, one Olivelands seven-year-old
girl wrote,
my eyes are the green of August.
I still see her eyes, her August, now.

Condors replenish. Phoenix, half-grown chick, survived Big Sur fire, matured,

fathered egg with Redwood Queen,
whose initial mate was lost to Dolan fire
all phoenix rise
blue-green egg until milky, milky way split
open up in some hollowed redwood, on cave floor dust, cliff edge

Once, my hand gleaned plume from cliff edge
something called me to reach in, feel
what left it gone fingers rake pulled from pit
what remnant left there.

Left there.

Let love lead.

Let hand that pummeled rest.

Let scowl rest, face relieve.

Let shoulders locked high, tight, recede.

Let feet cracked, worn, ease.

Let back, stiff, sore, bent open.

Let lungs swell breath like ocean.

Let all of us, all of us, all of us, let all of us be unbroken.

Take heart. Earth hears every tremble touch. Feels each foot. Listens now.
Bring her justice, protection, peace.

By the sixth, extinction translates to which way the wind blows, by seventh, species are temporary, expendable,
nothing matches life.

Abalone, White Point Conception, to Punta Abreojos
marine snail, mollusk, spiral, sea ear, mother, bowl
Albatross, short tailed
soaring on long, narrow wings, pink bill tipped bluish
Beetle, Casey's June
scarabs prefer alluvial fans, Sonoran desert scrub
Beetle, Mount Hermon June
Scarabaeidae in sandy soils Zayante Sand Hills
Butterfly, Behren's silverspot
upper golden under brown spotted silver/black
Butterfly, callippe silverspot
brushfoot hairy basal wing single annual flight
Butterfly, El Segundo blue
lays on coast buckwheat flowers, pollen nurtured
Butterfly, Lange's metalmark
from riverine sand dune, buckwheat bound
Butterfly, lotis blue
one-inch wingspans southwestern edge northern blue
Butterfly, mission blue
lay dorsal side lupine leaves
Butterfly, Myrtle's silverspot
lay on *viola* only, golf threatened
Butterfly, Palos Verdes blue
fog-shrouded, cool hills
Butterfly, Quino checkerspot
low-flying flutterer once most common
Butterfly, San Bruno elfin
swollen succulents entice
Butterfly, Smith's blue
dire, decimated from off-roading, livestock
Chub, bonytail

dark above, light below, desert fish
Chub, Owens tui
chunky, dorsal olive, bluish below
Condor, California
soar glide without wingbeat
we attended first return in the eighties
here, carried, deep in mind's eye—free
Crayfish, Shasta
dual swimmerets over volcanic rubble
Fairy shrimp, conservancy
complex wave-like legs beat
Fairy shrimp, longhorn
large stalked eyes, compound
Fairy shrimp, Riverside
vernal pool habitat, eggs tolerate heat, drought
Fairy shrimp, San Diego
seasonal rainfall dwellers
Flycatcher, southwestern willow
environmental degradation threatens
passerine, perching bird, yellow lower mandible
Fly, Delhi Sands flower-loving
Inland Empire, green-eyed
first fly listed endangered
extinction brinked
Fox, San Joaquin kit
smallest North American dog
petroleum threatened
Fox, San Miguel Island
Channel Islands, no wilds remain
Fox, Santa Catalina Island
longest tail, largest size
Fox, Santa Cruz Island
dine on summer holly, rose, cholla,
sumac, nightshade, deer mice, birds, crickets
Fox, Santa Rosa Island

golden eagles threaten, scarce

Frog, mountain yellow-legged Northern

cryptic coloration, splotches like lichen

Frog, mountain yellow-legged Southern

variable dorsal pattern, lacks vocal sacs

Frog, Sierra Nevada yellow-legged

shorter legged, eats dead

generations go at once if water dries

fewer frogs found, fewer grow legs, loose tails

thrive

Goby, tidewater
Grasshopper, Zayante band-winged
Kangaroo rat, Fresno
Kangaroo rat, giant
Kangaroo rat, Morro Bay
Kangaroo rat, San Bernardino Merriam's
Kangaroo rat, Stephen's
Kangaroo rat, Tipton
Lizard, blunt-nosed leopard
Mountain beaver, Point Arena
Mouse, Pacific pocket
Mouse, salt marsh harvest
Pikeminnow, Colorado
Pupfish, desert
Pupfish, Owens
Rabbit, riparian brush
Rail, California clapper
Rail, light-footed clapper
Rail, Yuma clapper
Salamander, California tiger, Santa Barbara
Salamander, California tiger, Sonoma
Salamander, desert slender
Salamander, Santa Cruz long-toed
Salmon, coho
Sea turtle, leatherback
Sheep, Peninsular bighorn
Sheep, Sierra Nevada bighorn
Shrew, Buena Vista Lake ornate
Shrike, San Clemente loggerhead
Shrimp, California freshwater
Skipper, Carson wandering
Skipper, Laguna Mountains
Snail, Morro shoulderband
Snake, San Francisco garter
Steelhead, Southern California DPS
Stickleback, unarmored threespine
Sucker, Lost River
Sucker, razorback

Sucker, shortnose
quapdo, *recover, recover*
Tadpole shrimp, vernal pool
shielded carapace, predate fish
Tern, California least
millinery trade decimated
Tiger beetle, Ohlone
instars hatch green jewels
Toad, arroyo
sandy streamsides seal
Tui chub, Mohave
sole endemic Mojave River fish
Vireo, least Bell's
riparian, moth eater
Vole, Amargosa
salt cedar your nemesis, invasive

Whale, blue
Mysticeti, largest giant
heart big as bear
sacrificed for plastic
Whale, finback
giant second to blue
entanglement, vessel strike
unnatural sound impends
Whale, humpback
compose love songs, sing
serenade serenade serenade
slap water's surface drumming
breach dance, leap to fly
Whale, Sei
leave only fluke prints
Whale, sperm
paddle flippers
dive deep, nap,
stand to sleep

Wolf, gray
avoiding humans, return
of their own volition

Woodrat, riparian
dusky-footed woodrat
gray, cinnamon fur
tails furred, not scaly

Beetle, delta green ground
metallic, bronze, green jewels
grassland-playa pool matrix

Beetle, valley elderberry longhorn
Central Valley riparian forests
decimated, threatened

Butterfly, bay checkerspot
caterpillars eat purple owl's clover

Butterfly, Oregon silverspot
early blue-violet hosts

Cuckoo, yellow-billed Western
ku-ku-ku-ku-ku-kowip-kowip-
kowip-kowip neotropical migrant

Fairy shrimp, vernal pool
swim on backs, stroking eleven leg sets

Frog, California red-legged
largest Western native frog

Frog, Oregon spotted
upturned chartreuse eyes

Gnatcatcher, coastal California
flicks, hops tiny range, habitat now suburbs

Lizard, Coachella Valley fringe-toed
Blow sand ecosystem dependent

Lynx, Canada contiguous U.S. SPS
tufted ear tipped, bobtail
habitat stripped now suburbs

Moth, Kern primrose sphinx
stout diurnal moth eat baby blue-eyes
during drought go underground

Murrelet, marbled
exists in pairs, fish crustaceans

Otter, southern sea
oil spills recalculate lifespan

Owl, northern spotted
nocturnal, monogamous,
reside in older forests

Plover, western snowy Pacific coastal pop
buff, pale, pocket-sized shorebird on open beach

Salamander, California tiger
prefers in-ground burrows

Salmon, Chinook California Coastal
coastal stream deterioration

Salmon, So. Oregon coho—No. Cal Coast
dam construction, habitat degradation

Seal, Guadalupe fur
loss to hooking, entanglement, oil spills, development

Sea turtle, olive ridley
olive-green heart-shaped shell
fishing gear, climate change, egg thieves

Smelt, delta
San Francisco Bay Delta degradation
smelt-down in the delta, ecosystem unravels

Snake, giant garter
sometimes infused with orange

Sparrow, San Clemente sage
dark streaks, dark cheeks
pigs, goats, military, cats

Steelhead, Central California Coast DPS
anadromous central coast riparian trout
climate change exacerbating issue
with dams, degradation

Steelhead, Northern California Coast DPS
winter / summer runs, stream temperature sensitivity

Sturgeon, green Southern DPS
can live to sixty, swimming marine
to fresh

Sucker, Santa Ana, three CA river basins
Seven Oaks Dam on the Santa Ana damaged habitat

Sucker, Warner
slender bodied, in shallow pools

Toad, Yosemite
warty skin, stocky, thick
can live twelve to fifteen years

Tortoise, desert, Mojave & Sonoran Deserts
columnar legs enjoy creosote bush flats
habitat destruction and poaching
leading to decline

Towhee, Inyo California
oldest known twelve years
ten months when banded
build nests in poison oak
dine on its pale white berries
feral burro foraging threatens

Trout, Lahontan cutthroat
stream spawner
endemic in Eastern California

Trout, Little Kern golden
olive to brass, flanks spotted
endemic in California, in isolation

early settlers transplanted
hybridization threatening existence
Trout, Paiute cutthroat
blush alongside your body
cattle graze, human recreation
subdue small stream network
Whipsnake, Alameda
human sprawl taking
taking, taking, taking
yellow racing striped
speeding shrub, chaparral
rodenticides, pesticides
herbicides, poison, poison

Little Kern golden trout,
rainbow overwhelms you.
All the caddis flies in Tulare
won't bring strength to tide.

Recently extinct:

California grizzly (*Ursus arctos californicus*) 1922

was shot in Tulare County, California

1924, grizzly maybe seen
Sequoia National Park

never again seen in California.

Their native state.

State seals, flags bear Monarch

Bear Flag Revolt in Sonoma settlers wiped out the grizzly, uzamati

Red star, lone supergiant, Betelgeuse
supernova

what happens when stars die
death of a star death of a star

Sacramento Valley tiger beetle
Southern California kit fox

Clear Lake splittail
Tecopa pupfish
Thicktail chub

Mono Lake diving beetle
Pasadena freshwater shrimp
Sooty crayfish
Xerces blue butterfly

Remembering the lives before them, we
broke into double-throated song scales
singing

nothing matches life,
recite their names now:

Ramshaw Meadows abronia
San Mateo thorn-mint
San Diego thorn-mint
Cushenbury oxytheca
San Clemente Island bird's-foot trefoil
Santa Cruz Island bird's-foot trefoil
Santa Cruz Island lotus
Blasdale's bent grass / delisted
Munz's onion
Yosemite onion
Sonoma alopecurus
San Diego ambrosia
large-flowered fiddleneck
McDonald's rockcress
Baker's manzanita

The Cedars manzanita
Santa Rosa Island manzanita
Little Sur manzanita / delisted
Franciscan manzanita
Del Mar manzanita
Hearsts' manzanita
San Bruno Mountain manzanita
Presidio manzanita
Morro manzanita
lone manzanita
Pacific manzanita
pallid manzanita
marsh sandwort
Humboldt milk-vetch
Cushenbury milk-vetch
Braunton's milk-vetch
Clara Hunt's milk-vetch
Lane Mountain milk-vetch
Long Valley milk-vetch
Coachella Valley milk-vetch
Fish Slough milk-vetch
Sodaville milk-vetch
Peirson's milk-vetch
Mono milk-vetch
Ventura Marsh milk-vetch
coastal dunes milk-vetch
Trask's milk-vetch
triple-ribbed milk-vetch
San Jacinto Valley crownscale
Bakersfield smallscale
Encinitas baccharis
bensoniella
Nevin's barberry
island barberry
Sonoma sunshine
Point Reyes blennosperma
dwarf goldenstar
Hoffman's rockcress

thread-leaved brodiaea
Kaweah brodiaea
Chinese Camp brodiaea
Indian Valley brodiaea
leafy reed grass
Dunn's mariposa lily
Siskiyou mariposa lily
Tiburon mariposa lily
Mariposa pussypaws
Stebbins' morning-glory
San Benito evening primrose
white sedge
Tompkins' sedge
tree-anemone
Tiburon paintbrush
succulent owl's-clover
ash-gray paintbrush
Mt. Gleason paintbrush
San Clemente Island paintbrush
soft-leaved paintbrush
Pitkin Marsh paintbrush
California jewel-flower
slender-pod jewel-flower / delisted
Coyote ceanothus
Hearsts' ceanothus
maritime ceanothus
Mason's ceanothus
Vail Lake ceanothus
Pine Hill ceanothus
Catalina Island mountain-mahogany
Santa Lucia purple amole
Camatta Canyon amole
salt marsh bird's-beak
soft bird's-beak
palmate-bracted bird's-beak
Howell's spineflower
Orcutt's spineflower
San Fernando Valley spineflower

Ben Lomond spineflower
Monterey spineflower
Scotts Valley spineflower
robust spineflower
Sonoma spineflower
Ashland thistle
fountain thistle
Chorro Creek bog thistle
Suisun thistle
surf thistle
La Graciosa thistle
Presidio clarkia
Vine Hill clarkia
Merced clarkia
Pismo clarkia
Springville clarkia
Mt. Diablo bird's-beak
seaside bird's-beak
Pennell's bird's-beak
Wiggins' croton
bristlecone cryptantha
July gold
Red Rock tarplant
Livermore tarplant
Otay tarplant
Gaviota tarplant
Santa Susana tarplant
Mojave tarplant
Baker's larkspur
Cuyamaca larkspur
golden larkspur
San Clemente Island larkspur
Mount Laguna aster
Vandenberg monkeyflower
beach spectaclepod
slender-horned spineflower
Cuyamaca Lake downingia
Santa Clara Valley dudleya

short-leaved dudleya
Agoura Hills dudleya
Santa Monica dudleya
Santa Cruz Island dudleya
Conejo dudleya
Laguna Beach dudleya
Santa Barbara Island dudleya
Verity's dudleya
Ash Meadows daisy
Kern mallow
Big Bear Valley sandwort
Santa Ana River woollystar
Hoover's woolly-star / FDR (gray, no note)
Tracy's eriastrum
Parish's daisy
Indian Knob mountainbalm
Lompoc yerba santa
Trinity buckwheat
lone buckwheat
Irish Hill buckwheat
Butterworth's buckwheat
conejo buckwheat
Santa Barbara Island buckwheat
San Nicolas Island buckwheat
Kellogg's buckwheat
southern mountain buckwheat
Cushenbury buckwheat
Thorne's buckwheat
Twisselmann's buckwheat
Congdon's woolly sunflower
San Mateo woolly sunflower
San Diego button-celery
Loch Lomond button-celery
Delta button-celery
Contra Costa wallflower
Menzie's wallflower
Santa Cruz wallflower
Hoover's spurge

Mexican flannelbush

Roderick's fritillary

Borrego bedstraw

El Dorado bedstraw

sand gilia

Boggs Lake hedge-hyssop

Orcutt's hazardia

Algodones Dunes sunflower

Butano Ridge cypress

Marin western flax

rock lady

water howellia

Webber's ivesia

Contra Costa goldfields

coast yellow leptosiphon

Congdon's lewisia

western lily

Parish's meadowfoam

Point Reyes meadowfoam

Pine Hill flannelbush

Gentner's fritillary

striped adobe-lily

box bedstraw

San Clemente Island bedstraw

Hoffmann's slender-flowered gilia

Ash Meadows gumplant

island rush-rose

Santa Cruz cypress

Gowen cypress

Lake County western flax

Santa Cruz tarplant

Tahquitz ivesia

Burke's goldfields

beach layia

San Francisco lessingia

Mason's lilaeopsis

Pitkin Marsh lily

Baker's meadowfoam

Butte County meadowfoam
Sebastopol meadowfoam
San Clemente Island woodland star
Mariposa lupine
The Lassics lupine
Milo Baker's lupine
Nipomo Mesa lupine
Father Crowley's lupine
Tidestrom's lupine
Truckee barberry / delisted
San Clemente Island bush-mallow
Santa Cruz Island bush-mallow
Santa Cruz Island malacothrix
island malacothrix
willowy monardella
San Joaquin woollythreads
Gambel's water cress
spreading navarretia
few-flowered navarretia
many-flowered navarretia
Twisselmann's nemacladus
Colusa grass
Amargosa nitrophila
Kneeland Prairie pennycress
Dehesa nolina
Eureka Dunes evening-primrose
Antioch Dunes evening-primrose
Bakersfield cactus
California Orcutt grass
San Joaquin Valley Orcutt grass
hairy Orcutt grass
slender Orcutt grass
Sacramento Orcutt grass
Baja California birdbush
Gander's ragwort

Layne's ragwort
Geysers panicum
Dudley's lousewort
white-rayed pentachaeta

Lyon's pentachaeta
northern Channel Islands phacelia
Brand's star phacelia / (gray, no note)
Yreka phlox
San Bernardino Mountains bladderpod
whitebark pine
Yadon's rein orchid
San Francisco popcornflower
Calistoga popcornflower
North Coast semaphore grass
San Bernardino blue grass
Napa blue grass
San Diego mesa mint
Santa Lucia mint
Otay Mesa mint
Scotts Valley polygonum
Black Rock potentilla (gray, no notes)
Hickman's cinquefoil
Hartweg's golden sunburst
San Joaquin adobe sunburst
Tahoe yellow cress
small-leaved rose
adobe sanicle
rock sanicle
Lake County stonecrop
Red Mountain stonecrop (gray, no notes)
Santa Cruz Island winged-rockcress
Owens Valley checkerbloom
Cuesta Pass checkerbloom
Parish's checkerbloom

Keck's checkerbloom
Kenwood Marsh checkerbloom
bird-foot checkerbloom
Scadden Flat checkerbloom
Red Mountain catchfly
Metcalf Canyon jewel-flower
Tiburon jewel-flower
California seablite
California dandelion
slender-petaled thelypodium
Santa Ynez false lupine
Santa Cruz Island fringepod
Hidden Lake bluecurls
showy rancheria clover
Pacific Grove clover
Monterey clover
Greene's tuctoria
Crampton's tuctoria or Solano grass
Red Hills vervain
big-leaved crownbeard

Look at This Blue

Mutant blue-eyed coyotes chance mutation

baby blues in nine coyotes suggesting proliferation
silvery, brown-backed with icy blue eyes
antenna ears turning, satellite-like, hearing voles

Santa Cruz, Sacramento, Point Reyes
their apex predators mostly wolves,
mountain lions, or killed by humans
Here, they are thriving, hunting
blue eyed chance mutation

Amah Mutsun Land Trust
Restoring Indigenous knowledge and practices
to Popeloutchom ancestral homelands

restores role as environmental stewards
—surviving descendant families—
Indigenous people who survived the Santa Cruz and San Juan Bautista
missions

You think it's exhaustive now; this is partial recount.

Entire peoples missionized.

Father Serra founded, oversaw enslavement, torture, rape, murder, worked to death—average lifespan mission Indian once taken, was seven years, no matter arrival age. He celebrated the harvest of souls of Indian children dying of European diseases in his captivity.

Saint?

Seven-year lifespan, no matter age of missionization. Worked to death and/or typhoid.

"Although the stated goal of the Missions was to return land to the Indians, no land was ever provided. During the Mission period over 19,421 Indians died at Mission San Juan Bautista and approximately 150,000 Indians died in California." —*Amah Mutsun Tribal Band*

"Indians found drunk or vagrant were arrested on Sunday, imprisoned overnight in a corral, and convicted on Monday. Because few could afford to pay the fine, the jail was kept stocked full of potential laborers. . . . Unable to pay the fines for their convictions, the prisoners were auctioned off in the 'slave market.'" —Brendan C. Lindsay

"Los Angeles had its slave mart, as well as New Orleans and Constantinople—only the slave at Los Angeles was sold fifty-two times a year as long as he lived." —Horace Bell

"the City Marshal and his assistants . . . spend the Sabbath in arresting and imprisoning Indians, supposed to be drunk. . . . Now, we have no heart to do the Marshal the slightest prejudice, but this leading off Indians and locking them up over night, for the purpose of taking away one of their paltry dollars, seems to us a questionable act." —*Los Angeles Star*

Sutter's Gold Rush set stage for state
slaughter
Sacramento River bloodied red wash
typical, from lifeline ripped
from innocents, 600-800 Indians enslaved by him

keeping in line with conquistadors
Native murders, massacres, enslavement
began long before others were also perpetrated upon.

Native slavery in Florida, 1596, a drop in the well of manifest
rivering the continent—the whole of it—
forget the manmade Panama Canal. Consider the absolute length
enslavement, massacre, murder.

California, free-soil state upon statehood,
sold Indians as common practice still.

Indian Act of 1850, California legislature authorized arrests
of any *vagrant* Natives to be *hired out* to highest bidder.
Native children to be indentured, before a justice of the peace,
by any white persons who wished for laborers.

"The value of the captives depends upon age, sex, beauty, and usefulness," wrote Calhoun. "Good looking females, not having passed the 'sear and yellow leaf,' are valued from $50 to $150 each; males, as they may be useful, one-half less, never more."

"That a war of extermination will continue to be waged between the races until the Indian race becomes extinct must be expected," he told legislators in the second state of the state address in 1851. "While we cannot anticipate this result but with painful regret, the inevitable destiny of the race is beyond the power or wisdom of man to avert."

—Peter Hardeman Burnett, the state's first governor

Tenderloin mornings.
Someone took a shot at me before 9 a.m.
It's been two days since neighbors
shot over me, lying over you,
protecting you,
since Travelers Aid allowed me to
get here to take cover.
At least your father can't kill me now.
This passing car, mad at the world,
taking potshots, has poor aim,
or didn't mean to score.
Just trying to get some juice,
keep hydrated, my sister
still awake from her night shift
watching you for the first time
for ten minutes while I cross
Hyde, then Turk, grab a box of juice,
piece of bread, head back, unscathed.
Pass by the old man someone brought
from a reservation, left here
on the street. No one knows his
language. My sister says he'll accept
a sandwich, juice, so I go back, grab him one,
too. Today it's orange. *Here's a heel.* Someone
from St. Vincent's gave him a cane. He looks
maybe blind, or cataracted. Wish his name
was known. Wish we knew his home, get
him with his people. Morning seems
high above. The buildings block out
any rise and the whole thing seems
to spin cardinal points opposite
so north is south. Peninsula
living—Yelamu—Ramaytush,
Ohlone, my sister learns at SFSU,
works late shift, printing newspapers,

working for a bachelors in Native Studies,
takes her about eleven years complete.

Me, I'm scrambling just to hydrate, acclimate.
In the year Tom Petty wails, *I said,*
you don't have to live like a refugee.
Score before Care Not Cash SF labeled me indigent,
didn't offer a home, just rent to my sister.
In a few weeks you'll have red measles,
not move for days, dehydrated, will nearly
leave. From me standing in line, St. Vincent's,
with you wrapped tightly in sling alongside,
for food, medicine, essentials we don't keep.
The stream of morning over your face,
when you recover.

We're 7th/8th gen
shirttails undeserving,

unenrolled unfit undocumented
two gens from fluencies,

heritage,
but the Friendship House reps say we're welcome
to sit in if we get over Oakland way.

This is before I could express
myself. Chin still positioned,
ready. Or chin down, ghosting
into horizons you can't see here.

My sister came here in the
seventies. Our mom and dad
for their honeymoon after
blind-date meeting in San Diego
in late forties. Last century.
You can feel them here, still.
Each time it's real, we call,
note space, *yes, we were there.*

Before any time passes, we
realize other families don't
have these homing knowns.

My sister is embarrassed of me.
Too backwoods. Too field laborer.
Too sharecropping. Too fisher.
Too farmer. Too backwoods.
Mocks my handiwork. Asks if
I plan to sell trinkets on the
side of the road. Maybe leather-
work, I claim. Show her mine.

She walks a block ahead of me
mocking me to her city friends.
Like we walked aisles over
from our mom, deep in delusion,
cursing through aisles in Piggly Wiggly,
but never mocking her. Not once.
Where did this mocking come from?
Raven cry (for my heart).

Here, streets lined with fresh
refugees, straggler homeless, cardboard
box men, prostitutes, pimps, beautiful
neighborhood people who teach me
you can get a great meal for $2 on
this block. How to eat with chopsticks,
which store gives free bread if you
don't have $. Lots of Skins pass through.
Not Ohlone.

Indian Country, California, every bit.

Under U.S. law,
over a hundred rancherias, reserved spaces, trust allotments
more than ribbon state fabric, more original weave

No other state has more original peoples residing
one-hundred-nine nations, federal recognition
seventy-eight petitioners

Genocide did not begin at the rush for gold.
Spanish missionaries, settlers, ranchers

Still, estimates of fatalities exist:
300,000 to 250,000 Spanish-rule killed
250,000 to 150,000 under Mexico
Under US, after 1848

in two years of gold fever, 100,000 killed.
of 150,000 people, 20,000 more killed in the next 25 years,
when *the state spent $1.7 million to murder*
16,000.
When the state—

When its mission missionized

How many villages could be missionized, enslaved for one mission?
Led by Father Junípero Serra
Father Estévan Tapís

Santa Inez Mission:
Achillimo, Aguama, Ahuamhoue, Akachumas, Akaitsuk, Alahulapgas, Alizway, Asiuhuil, Awashlaurk, Calahuasa, Cascel, Cholicus, Chumuchu, Coloc, Geguep, Guaislac, Huhunata, Hunawurp, lalamne, Ionata, Jonatas, Kalak, Kalawashuk, Katahuac, Kulahuasa, Kuyam, Matiliha, Mekewe, Mishtapawa, Nipoma, Nutonto, Sapelek, Saptuui, Sauchu, Shopeshno, Sikitipuc, Sisuchi, Situchi, Sotonoemu, Souscoc, Stucu, Suiesia, Suktanakamu, Tahijuas, Takuyumam, Talaxano, Tapanissilac, Tarkepsi, Tekep, Temesathi, Tequepis, Tinachi, Tsamala, Tujanisuissilac.

San Miguel Island:
Nimollollo, Zaco.

Santa Rosa Island:
Kshiwukciwu, Lilibeque, Muoc, Ninumu, Níquesesquelua, Niquipos, Patiquilid, Patiquiu, Pilidquay, Pisqueno, Poele, Siliwihi.

Santa Cruz Island:
Alali, Chalosas, Chosho, Coycoy, Estocoloco, Hahas, Hitschowon, Klakaamu, Lacayamu, Liyam, Macamo, Mashcal, Mishumac, Nanahuani, Niakla, Nichochi, Nilalhuyu, Nimatlala, Nimitapal, Nitel, Nomkolkol, Sasuagel, Xugua.

San Buenaventura Mission:
Aguin, Alloc, Anacbuc, Chihucchihui, Chumpache, Eshulup, Kachyayakuch, Kanwaiakaku, Kinapuke, Lacayamu, Liam, Lisichi, Lojos, Luupsch, Mahow, Malahue, Malico, Matilhja, Miguihui, Miscanaka, Piiru, Sespe, Shishalap, Simi. Sisa, Sisjulcioy, Sissabanonase, Soma, Tapo, Ypuc, Yxaulo.

Purísima Mission:
Alacupusyuen, Ausion, Esmischue, Esnispele, Espiiluima, Estait, Fax, Guaslaique, Huasna, Huenejel, Huenepel, Husistaic, Ialatnma, Jlaacs, Kachisupal, Lajuchu, Lipook, Lisahuats, Lompoc, Nahuey, Naila, Ninyuelgual, Nocto, Omaxtux Pacsiol, Paxpili, Sacsiol, Sacspili, Salachi, Sihimi, Silimastus, Silimi, Silino, Silisne, Sipuca, Sisolop, Sitolo, Stipu, Suntaho, Tutachro.

Santa Barbara Mission:
Alcax, Alican, Alpincha, Alwathalama, Amolomol, Anejue, Awhawhilashmu, Cajats, Cajpilili, Casalic, Cashwah, Chiuchin, Cholosoc, Chuah, Cinihuay, Cuyamus, Eleunaxciay, Eljman, Eluaxcu, Estuc, Geliac, Gleuaxcuqu, Guainonost, Guina, Hanava, Hello, Huelemin, Huililoc, Huixapapa, Humalija, Hunxapa, Inajalaihu, Inojey, Ipec, Ituc, Lagcay, Laycayamu, Lintja, Lisuchu, Lugups, Majalayghua, Mishtapalwa, Mistaughchewaugh, Numguelgar, Otenashmoo, Salpilel, Sayokinck, Sihuicom, Silpoponemew, Sinicon, Sisahiahut, Sisuch, Snihuax, Sopone, Taxlipu, Texmaw, Xalanaj, Xalou.

Miscellaneous:
Anacoat, Anacot, Antap, Aogni, Asimu, Bis, Caacat, Casnahacmo, Casunalmo, Cayeguas, Chwaiyok, Cicacut, Ciucut, Ciyuktun, Elquis, Escumawash, Garomisopona, Gun, Helapoonuch, Honmoyaushu, Hueneme, Humkak, Immahal, Isha, Ishgua, Kamulas, Kasaktikat, Kashiwe, Kashtok, Kashtu, Kaso, Katstayot, Kaughii, Kesmali, Koiyo, Kuiyamu, Lohastahni, Mahahal, Malhokshe, Malito, Malulowoni, Maquinanoa, Masewuk, Mershom, Michiyu, Micoma, Misesopano, Mishapsna, Misinagua, Mismatuk, Mispu, Mugu, Mupu, Nacbue, Nipomo, Nocos, Ojai, Olesino, Onkot, Onomio, Opia, Opistopia, Paltatre, Partocac, Potoltuc, Pualnacatup, Quanmugua, Quelqueme, Quiman, Salnahakaisiku, Sapaquonil, Saticoy, Satwiwa, Shalawa, Shalkahaan, Shisblaman, Sholikuwewich, Shuku, Shup, Shushuchi, Shuwalashu, Simomo, Sisichii, Sitaptapa, Siuktun, Skonon, Spookow, Sulapiu, Susuquey, Sweteti, Swino, Tallapoolina, Temeteti, Tocane, Topotopow, Tukachkach, Tushumu, Upop, Walektre, Wihatset, Xabaagua, Xagua, Xocotoc, Yutum.

Chumash Tribe
The Santa Rosa islanders, of the Chumashan family of California.

How many massacres?

Sacramento River Massacre
Klamath Lake Massacre
Sutter Buttes Massacre
Pauma Massacre
Temecula Massacre
Rancheria Tulea Massacre
Kern and Sutter Massacres
Konkow Maidu Slaver Massacre
Bloody Island Massacre
Mariposa War Massacre
Old Shasta Town Massacre
Bridge Gulch Massacre
Wright Massacre
Howonquet Massacre
Yontocket Massacre
Achulet Massacre
Ox Incident Massacre
Klamath River Massacres
Shingletown Massacre
Round Valley Settler Massacre
Jarboe's War Massacre
Pit River Massacre
Chico Creek Massacre
Massacre at Bloody Rock
Indian Island Massacre
Keyesville Massacre
Konkow Trail of Tears Massacre
Oak Run Massacre
Owens Lake Massacre
Three Knolls Massacre
Camp Seco Massacre
Kingsley Cave Massacre

Land of the—

war crimes, crimes against humanity, genocide

without limitations, statute.

Solution set out in Vizenor's
tribunals
assembled in the academy, investigated, fully researched trials, for the premeditated serial genocide committed through government role/s.

Call for country, accountability, justice.

California, California

A few cattle lost, probably killed by white men, began the basis of massacre.
State-sponsored—

1856–1859 *Round Valley Settler Massacres:*
White settlers killed 1000+ Yuki over three years in separate massacres.

1859–1860 *Jarboe's War:*
Eel River Rangers / white settlers led by Walter Jarboe killed
at least 283 Indian men
countless Indian women and children.

U.S. *Government reimburses their costs.*

1860 *Indian Island:*
80–250 Wiyot killed by white settlers in three near simultaneous assaults
Humboldt County, California. Mostly women, children, elders were
massacred.

1863 *Konkow Trail of Tears:*
August, 1863, Konkow Maidu ordered sent to Bidwell Ranch in Chico,
then to Round Valley Reservation at Covelo. Any remaining to be shot.
Rounded up and marched, west of Sacramento Valley 461 began the walk
277 finished on the 18th of September, 1863.

1864 *Oak Run Massacre: California settlers massacred 300 Yana*
gathered for spiritual ceremony near the head of Oak Run.

45 tribal communities of formerly recognized California tribes terminated in United States Termination policy in the 1950s.
Tribal communities never recognized by US.

In 1994, the state of California recognized the Tongva "as the aboriginal tribe of the Los Angeles Basin." Senate Bill 1134

2017, Governor Jerry Brown first California governor to acknowledge a state-sponsored genocide.

It's called a genocide. That's what it was. A genocide. [There's] no other way to describe it and that's the way it needs to be described in the history books. And so I'm here to say the following: I'm sorry on behalf of the state of California. 2019, Governor Gavin Newsom

Newsom also established a "truth and healing council" to provide Native perspectives on the historical record. The council will include tribal representatives and others and issue a report on the historical relationships between Native Californians and the state of California.

In 2020-2021, during the pandemic, COVID-19, former Yolo deputy sheriff, bigot, sponsors petition to recall Newsom.

The state's first legislative session gave white settlers the ability to take custody of Native children, arrest Native peoples at will and enslave them for petty "crimes."

For Indians and Indian Country there are special rules that govern state and local jurisdiction.
There may also be federal and tribal laws that apply.

Chinese Massacre

Golden Dragon Massacre

Thousand Oaks Shooting *San Ysidro McDonald's Massacre*

San Bernardino Attack

Pacific Air Lines Flight 773 Mass Murder-Suicide

California Genocide, 9492 to 16,094 killed in massacres

1846-1873 over 120,000 died overall during state sponsored period

California leads
mass pop-pop-pop

COVID-19 times
firings fell first year

come
worst to first
pandemic ratios

What's the gun-incident-ratio for falling illness?
First time someone placed
pistol grip in my hand
was roulette challenge

You?

How many times was I given up, left
for dead rejected objectified ejected
does it matter, still when

jump-started or just woke when unexpected to
always returning to the beauty of this world
abject misery layered still splendor despite
beautiful/horrendous juxtapositioning
throughout time

Look at This Blue

Mission blue butterfly *from coastal chaparral, grasslands,*
Mission District San Francisco, Twin Peaks, Marin County
most upon San Bruno Mountain
small, delicate gossamer-winged
male, iridescent blue-lavender
female, dark brown, blue base
fringed in long, white hair-like scales
undersides spotted
wingspread 1-1.5 inches
caterpillars solely ingest native California lupine,
eat silver, summer, varicolor lupine,
adults drink flower nectar, buckwheat, golden asters, wild hyacinths
endangered first by development;
public infrastructure development projects remain significant threat

The civil rights of nonwhites were so contentious that California failed to ratify the 14th and 15th Amendments—granting citizenship to former slaves and ensuring the rights of black men to vote—until the middle of the 20th century

California banned slavery in 1849. California law allowed
Native people to be enslaved in 1910.

1999, *Ishi's brain returned to his closest living relatives,*
the Yana people

Twenty-four immigrants have died in ICE *custody, by August* 2019,
during 45.

At least seven children since late 2018.

Since January 2019, *more than ninety people have died*
encountering US BORDER AGENTS. Three California related.

Over 130 *fatal encounters with* CBP *since* 2010

Use of the largest federal law enforcement entity
U.S. Customs and Border Protection (CBP)

Use of force
Use of ignorance
Use of weapons
Use of fascism
Use of projectiles
Use of asphyxiation
Use of taser
Use of fists
Use of feet
Use of chemical agent
Use of high-speed chase

Use of inadequate medical attention
Use of medical emergencies
Use of homicide
Use of fear
Use of aggression
Use of terror
Use of depression
Use of drowning
Use of heat
Use of cold
Use of privilege
Use of history
Use of future
Use of economics
Use of education
Use of power
Use of language
Use of literacy
Use of literature
Use of poverty
Use of situation
Use of attitude
Use of annoyance
Use of knee-jerk reaction
Use of anger
Use of weather
Use of water
Use of nutrition
Use of supplies
Use of pharmaceuticals
Use of essential needs
Use of shelter
Use of foreigner
Use of alien
Use of mistaken identity

Use of homecoming
Use of family visitation
Use of parental duty
Use of condition
Use of discretion
Use of fabrication
Use of collision
Use of withholding
Use of position
Use of brutality
Use of border crossing

Use of lack of conviction of any on-duty agent
  in the ninety-year history of the agency

She left her children
with her mother
He didn't have ID
They were in a car
Suspicious
Severe dehydration
She needed insulin
He had pneumonia
He had pneumonia
He had pneumonia
He needed heart medicine
He had a seizure
  after agents secured him
reportedly
Children in border detention
  have contracted Coronavirus
reportedly
20,427 total confirmed COVID-19 cases
  in border custody, facility
1,025 in current isolation

reportedly
They were turned away while
attempting to donate diapers, hygienic supplies,
sanitizers, toys, toothbrushes, books, clothing,
masks, gloves, bottled water
The agent spiked water jugs
left for asylum seekers crossing desertways
The second agent flipped them
emptying the contents
He was in the middle of a divorce
when he shot the migrant teen
They were Salvadoran
She was Honduran
He was Guatemalan

They were Indian American
She was Cuban
He was American
She was Mexican
He was Congolese
They were Nicaraguan
She was Colombian
Nationality unknown unknown unknown
She was Canadian
He was a U.S. citizen
She was an American citizen
He was a long-term California resident
In the case of brutality
Officer logged in fear of life
No weapon was found
Two were alleged suicides
Failure to provide adequate care
Shot in the back twice, then killed
by the border agent
The teen was noted as seriously ill
when they locked him in, secured the cell

Shot and killed standing on the bank throwing rocks
Foot chased into the lake, they drowned there
Shot multiple times in the back for throwing rocks
for insubordination
He was taken to a holding cell following arrest
in six hours he was dead

"I want David Villalobos' name out there," said his younger sister,
Brittany Villalobos. "I want it out there and I want there to be noise."

their names

All along the wall Indigenous remains were unearthed from centuries of rest
we are restless

Not breaking this up for comfort.

She remembered stories, grandmas watching over
from long ago. Still here, singing comfort –

Evening, on the chaparral

rain-soaked creosote releases smoky scent
lingers under Pleiades, coming up on buck moon.

Our governess, she reduces inflammation,
rids fungus, her twigs, bark, teas
hold mysteries, toxins, medicinal

properties, unfenced, unwalled, growing
for anyone to reap, moon lights her tips like

Pleiades, seven little goats, little eyes, seven sisters,
Subaru, pearls, hen with chicks, united.
Taken there, held, or forever running from maddened machismo,
forever unchecked – forever.

Rainy stars, sailing stars, mapping out navigation
accompanied by dual forces, often parental,
one turns invisible at will.

She was invisible for a while.
Headlined for an hour
between the lists of COVID-19 deaths, hospitalizations,
cases soaring in encampments, detentions,
between borders, nations, between worlds – hope.

Kids running from agents, she lost her way, step,
before being thrown into the freezer
assigned foil for blanket, shivering through shimmering night.

Mama

Lodged in the spine.
Lodged in the neck.
Lodged in the abdomen.
Lodged in the skull.

Unlodged, slept on concreted curb.
Unlodged, covered themselves with creosote branches.
Unlodged, pulled shirt over head to sleep.
Unlodged, they expired.

State of the State.
Homelessness increased remarkably

If we were only Otay Mountain lotus
  butterflies, maybe

why did you come
we love California
our spouses are here
our children
grandmothers
work
our lives

His country of origin
        Vietnam
admitted as lawful, permanent resident
        1984
final order of removal
        2004
        2005
released on supervision
        2017
found guilty of disorderly conduct
  upon imprisonment, denied medical issue
was taking prescription for schizophrenia
  for major depressive disorder
        2018
transferred, unresponsive, no reflexes, gag or pupils

The preliminary cause of death was myocardial infarction
  multiple blocked arteries

The Armenian married to a U.S. citizen, was pronounced dead.
The preliminary cause of death is
hypertensive and atherosclerotic
cardiovascular disease, and the manner of
death was natural

The video findings of the final days of a sixteen-year-old
  do not match the agents' account

How much does a short story earn a writer?

California on Friday sued the Trump administration to challenge the legality of a new "public charge" rule that could deny green cards to immigrants who receive public assistance, including food stamps, Medicaid and housing vouchers.
August 2019, LA Times

California and 19 other states sue over rule under 45
allowing prolonged detention for asylum
seekers—August 2019

Held anyway without consent, mutually fit, nothing but wrong.

My gut aches. All this, all this indelible hurt.

A scrub jay calls for peanuts, whole, raw, shell intact.
Each year a pair leaves one, takes one with. Our bird stays,
plays with squirrels, takes nuts from us, coexists.

Trusts.

Where is the love for young ones taken, without reason, hope?

Machine state racking up torture tendencies, kids dying inside
the State, not inside the state. California over rule, overrule.
Find freedom for all. Housing for all. Education for all. Make this
a free state despite the State.

For 50th time, California sues the Trump administration—
"That's a lot of lawsuits" —*California Attorney General Xavier Becerra*

The lawsuits range from fighting the diversion of emergency dollars to fund a border wall and environmental protection rollbacks, as well as contesting the dismantling of the Affordable Care Act and banning transgender people from the military. —May 2019, *Sacramento Bee*

Trump sued California on Tuesday over a new law requiring presidential candidates to release their tax returns to run in the state's primary elections. —August 2019, Reuters

"A 2,000-mile wall is a monument to stupidity, not just vanity, to stupidity," Newsom said. "It's pure political theater. He creates these sideshows, this political theatre, this political grandstanding." —California Governor Gavin Newsom, March 2019, CBS Los Angeles

California has joined with 21 other states, the District of Columbia, Los Angeles, and five other cities in a legal challenge to the Trump administration's repeal of Obama-era clean power rules.

"This is not just about fighting Donald Trump," said Newsom. "This is about our kids and our grandkids. This is about clean air, clean water and endangered species." —KQED

Glacial melt, waves and waves.
100 times faster than previously imagined.
Ice, half the planet away, sheets
lost on edges of continents
rise levels, half a meter more
massive accelerating increase
1.5 millimeters per year plus this new ice melt

We're all sitting on ground near enough what might go under, liquify,
on what used to be an ocean, could be
shells still testify—

Four bodies found floating from dive-boat fire
Twenty more below the deck
dozens missing, lost.
Channel Islands Labor Day cruise—
Conception burned while mooring.

Crew, awake, jumped to safety.
My son was on that boat, someone said.

Conducting shoreline searches for any new survivors.
No one is calling out; it is still, quiet.
The *Grape Escape* helping rescue.

Asked if crew tried to help passengers, *I don't have answers.*
The call was garbled, it was not clear.
Mayday. The boat fully ablaze.

Bow still visible
vessel sank in sixty-four feet of water.
3:15 a.m., the call came.

Antarctica counts for 10% of all ocean level rise.
Greenland 20%.
somewhere highly crevassed ice is falling.
On ice summit, rain met ice
first fall recorded. First touch.

Glaciers sitting below sea level, breaking off, breaking.
hard to find open air
in the midst of so many glacial breaks, floating by.

Glaciers flowing directly into oceans.
Their component, contribution
to rising levels.
El Niño can worsen flooding, disrupt wetlands.
Rise

the prophesied child, boy, one of 270,000 shelterless California K-12 kids
last year, the first of COVID-19,
his hand shot through, shot, playing where he lives, camp,
Oakland, land of acorn mush, hush

don't remember the times tumbles whirred to stop
to sleep warm, when washers left
climb in, pull door to, hope nobody closes tight
night

absence barred souls
locked up slept despair measled
slung like bundles
like this boy his chin positioned to scoop
day away like any other, this year, this draw, this whittled life

restrained on his stomach five minutes
pinned by Alameda police
gone gone

You were so sick, so internally embattled
suddenly a soft touch to the shoulder
ghost, maybe, until you glimpsed the opossum's so-soft front foot
offering solace, companionship
touch in the time of despair

mercy mercy *woah-ah mercy mercy*
me

Perforating heart, lung, liver
Los Angeles County Coroner—shot twice—
woah mercy mercy

Storm swell, high tide, soak
surge significant seawater over coast,
pushed waters over coastal riprap

the ocean's going to win.
Caught by a strong wave
once went out so far, so deep, couldn't see

surface from bottom, shore was mystery. Spectacular waves loose—
1989 Loma Prieta earthquake
will be less costly than 2025 rise.

It's all leaving. Divers sleep in a single room of bunk beds none of them in sight.

Shots fired at panga boat, smuggling
marijuana into a legal state, illegally
bales overboard, still searching.

A bill requires training for officers in
de-escalating confrontations

power line to a tower fail

in known wind conditions.

Lawsuits for Pacific Gas & Electric, in wildfires

faulty equipment, negligence made.
Surveillance

Poway synagogue, Gilroy Garlic Festival,
semiautomatic, he cut through fence to
kill

horrific, gun-violence epidemic
San Fernando man shot his family
parents, brother, friend a bus
Poway, a rabbi shot in both hands, AR-15
woman protecting him killed
shrapnel, a bit of twisted irony.

Look at This Blue

Blue Whale *alongside Monterrey, San Diego, Baja*
gentle giant heaviest animal to ever live on earth, twice
Argentinosaurus
ship strikes kill eleven per year, U.S. West Coast, with ship increase
population will be depleted, noise, military testing, sonic battery,
chemicals, plastics
krill, anchovy, tiny fish, tiny crustaceans absorb
microplastics
a blue whale eats between two and four tons
of krill per day

—blue with belly full of plastics—

Indian children traded, sold

bid, early 1900 a law still refused

difference between apprenticeship
slavery

Indian children unprotected under any laws

special laws written to master

Children's home means any institution, dwelling, house, tent.

(1890), the California Supreme Court ruled that public school
districts in California may not establish separate schools
for children of African descent.

(1890) Mr. Horatio N. Rust was instructed by the Commissioner of Indian Affairs

to find a suitable site in Southern California
for an Indian school, separate from other
children
and their own families
Perris Indian School opened 1892
became Sherman Institute 1903

1971 became accredited and known as Sherman Indian High School

Those who died there were often buried in the school cemetery.

*May 3 marks an old tradition amongst the local
tribes where many local reservations decorate
their cemeteries with flowers and replace old
crosses. Sherman Indian High School designates
this as Indian Flower Day*

he fell under freight train during escape
typhoid ended them
broken heart
broken

In 1852, California legislators passed a harsh fugitive slave law that condemned dozens of African American migrants to deportation and lifelong slavery.

THE CHINESE EXCLUSION ACT OF 1882 was signed into law on May 6, 1882.

"An act to execute certain treaty stipulations relating to Chinese"

prohibited the immigration of Chinese laborers for ten years.

Deprived, defrauded,
their property embezzled for trains, cars, buses,
planes, expended
to deport people from the neighborhood, with no due cause,
no right to due process, no justice under the law.

Beginning in 1929, the State of California forcibly removed
400,000 Mexican American people
from their state,
their country of birth. Enacting threats, committing
violent acts, raiding targeted persons,
misnaming them illegal aliens,
despite legal residence, citizenship.

This chapter may be cited as the
"Apology Act for the 1930s Mexican Repatriation Program." 8721.

The Legislature finds and declares

for the fundamental violations
of their basic civil liberties and constitutional rights committed during the period of illegal deportation and coerced emigration.

The State of California apologizes

The State of California
regrets
the suffering and hardship endured as a direct result of the government sponsored Repatriation

The State defamed, robbed, banished neighbors
so many places counted the hours, days, years, most often there, became
silhouette lines in Griffith Park, Tule Lake, Manzanar,
bags tagged Woodland, Turlock, Tulare, Stockton,
rations read San Bruno, Salinas, Sacramento,
babies born Pomona, Pinedale, Owens Valley,
elders passed Merced, Fresno, Arcadia, or loaded on trains, departed –
Like horses, left in Santa Anita Racetrack stables, Tanforan racetrack
—Tanforan–8033 detained, interned.
Tanforan nights spent on haysack beds, stinky stalls, rank from manure.
Miné fresh from exhibiting and curating in San Francisco MoMA
Here, her UC Berkeley MA, art/anthropology
documented detainees in charcoal, watercolor, tempura.
1912, born/raised Riverside, California. Banned from living on the west coast, 1942.
Executive Order 9066: Resulting in the Relocation of Japanese
Citizen 13660
Miné Okubo, Nisei

The fat cats she offered, a glimpse of humanity to calm despair.

Citizen 13660 (1946)—*American Book Award* (1984)

The Civil Liberties Act of 1988, *Restitution for World War II internment of Japanese-Americans and Aleuts*

apologize on behalf of the people
discourage injustices
make restitution

to citizens, resident aliens, Aleuts of Pribilof Islands
for all taken, taken, taken, taken, occupied, or destroyed

discourage future violations of civil liberties
Make credible, make sincere, concern

In the field, forced to crawl through culvert, water neck-high, floating
no way to maneuver, with a child through this

to escape immersion, criminals, violence, to find peace
find home, find dreaming.

Like clouds pulling into towers, we gathered,
all of us. They made us throw out the suitcase
we brought, made us leave the known

empty ourselves, for something promised
now a threat. I remember spare-changing with him on second floor
watching that I bring enough in.

Your earnest face. Asking me, "Where is he?"
"How about you and I leave, I buy you a dinner, you get away?"
My emptiness void of belief such was real,

"Even a quarter?" hand extended.
I still think of you sometimes.

When he busted my face, oftentimes, my diligence went unnoticed.
When he claimed I was in car wrecks
his mom believed.
Nearly killed me in one, so must be
must be a car wreck every other week, each time
purple faded, teeth repaired, gauze removed
bruised from brow to jaw, pummeled
what a mess

Those who rage are full of emptiness, hollow people, unfilled, vacant.
Hate fulfills the space, festers there, blooms.
Vacancy blinked neon in motor court windows
like his eyes, heart, was it a heart? No heart.

Something in me could care less now. Something in my rearranged appearance
fits my unfittedness, signals *this one can be* don't be fooled,
I have a way out.

In the bus on the way to retraining for field workers.
We left Santa Paula for Ventura daily.

Rhododendron, eucalyptus, Limoneira orange groves, peppers,
flowers for Burpee Seed Company
red-winged hawks every mile
of eucalyptus 126 Ventura Highway
on watch, like us, for movement.

x

Santa Paula. North star of Guanajuato.
Mupu of Chumash.
We escaped here. Refugees. Closed eyes,
let finger configure map, conjure home. This is where.
From here everything changes. Rewrite, reset, reverb.
Offer projects for Santa Ynez kids at get-go. Offer self.
Send for my folks to follow. Dad notes, know this—
if there is snow on Topatopa, everything's okeh.

Mom doesn't leave the pickup until the fourth day.
Vallejo apartment, their last place West Coast. Way prior
to my lifetime.

Restful now, restart. Gratitude.
So lucky to have had a dad.

Vista del Mar
resort asylum we deliver
her
to begin anew life I
picked lock when she bolted
drove her north to find peace midst
schizophrenia with California persuasion
first time in facility without a state embrace.
first time without electroshock, without abuse, without malice there
where we left her
so many times
Here she begins
new

Your father released from prison
for voice-modulated arson tell-all.
He would knock over someone, something,
force me into a car to drive him
we would be chased, careen, pulled over,
he would jump out with sawed-offs ready
walk straight up to them
tell them what they would tell their dispatch
and they would.

I never knew him before he assaulted me.

Your arm was twisted, bone exposed
face past point of wet stained,
fledgling fell there

"He wouldn't stop crying, so he's been sitting here since lunch."

That was the final day you were left-prominent
all bland shaming, "Big boys don't use their left hand"
"The class scissors are made for right-hands"
suddenly would satisfy same teacher who marched you
here and complained about the noise
after the class favorite broke your arm on monkey bars.

Like me, when the boy sucker round-housed me coming around hall corner.
Upper force, lifted me off, hard land on knee moved the cap
blood everywhere from fully laid out nose
first teacher on the scene, invokes surname, "clean up this mess."

Schools were made to break us.

Santa Paula Bank on Harvard, was it?

Dad, deaf, spoke out loud, *Where did everyone go?*

while tellers duck, cover.

While robber

displays his weapon to me, gestures at my toddler,

suggest I gather.

I motion toward Dad

gesturing his deafness, offer to gather him as well,

mercy, with peace,

from the bank robber who escapes on a bicycle

about the time tellers

remember him from high school.

On Jurupa a bike laid flat, crashed out
up against curb
just below his awkwardly posed corpse
was the sense of it
something crude, a twisting, limb thrusting rigid, blue—
spread out in some complex tangle, unnatural
under sign for childcare center thirty feet from his fall.
He must have flipped there, over handlebars
like a child might, striking concrete too fast, too hard,
this man maybe heart attack, maybe assaulted.
his clothes worn, raggedy, last testament, homeless, maybe.
We moved to prayer in moment, called 9-1-1,
begged for mercy

begged for peace, sympathy for miserable
the river-bottom people begged
for when we were them

scruffed, scuffed, sleeping under overpass, in dryers
to keep warm, kids, we were
under shattered skies,
dogs licking our faces, all we knew of love, here.
Each Chihuahua, every four-legged,
under arms, held close

every homeless leaning into shade in swelter
we worry about water
are they slaked?

"I'm fifty years old. I have MS. They beat me up."
he offers when
we insist he come order a sandwich with us
Subway counter
"Can I get a bag of chips, a drink?"
his eye so neglected
I throw my arms around him, hug him, sisterly,
mujer at register begins to cry
We carry his order to table,
his legs fully turned in at knees, feet uncooperative
not even a shuffle to them, just laborious plow.

I plead with him to go to City Hall for help, for immediate need programs
"I don't know who to ask. I can't get around."

We eat. I send love through my skin, eyes, insisting.
It's not enough, buy sandwich, give advice.
Late at night, I weep for him, for all of us who don't fit
for vacuous disparity between beauty / pain.

—all those nights spent under trestles when it was me that way—

He called while she was dying. Vista Cove, Santa Paula,
demanding her war widow's pension,
said he needed boots,

more like boot up.

All we could think of was how he beat her, called her Dog.
Trampled her.

She begged us to wire—
The courts had never allowed us
monetary control as her conservators
this one last time, we just pretended, bought her another day here.

In honor of the woman who loved children so much
she forced the city to put in a crosswalk
for grade school kids crossing, running late, between cars—
who might fall down be hit—

Glen City Elementary, nearly thirty years later,
Remembered— called
for family members to attend a play

little ones there now
so moved they chose the story to make their own homage
in tribute to a Santa Paula hero.

You went with your grandpa, brought me last lines,

So she could look out her window and see them safely cross
every day.

Something anyone might do—

Here in shadows, leaves
keep life close, fruit the taste of it, dusk, following plant

rows around crates, comfort here, home
nothing like a bed under stars
when we need.

Gleam now in rain slickening
arroyo willow branch
as blue elderberry summon
wind, Santa Anas
tangle reason, still leaves night
in bang by owl wing.

Here, hammocked over
oasis watering life,
rocks form mouths
predawn, calling.

Deep in night, corded sky ropes
tug through visceral root
harness reckoning, throttle
to timbre
thrum, strum, pluck gut sleeve
kindle fiddle full belly
flourish poppies as quarter notes
spiral double helix
high above California fan palm
until stars are born.

Joshua Trees of the first vandalized during
shutdown, national park defunding

1,200 square miles at risk
high desert, 45 might as well have burned it all
rangy succulent majesty
said to straddle Mojave and Colorado Deserts,
incoming spray-painting rocks,
smiley face, THE 419, three underscores
felling Joshuas to make off-roading roads,
so they could drive into sensitive areas
where vehicles are banned
by 2100 climate change rising temperatures
may take it all, they're hurrying along.
People climbed the massive junipers to break
branches for prohibited fires, it's welcome shade
now gone.

"There is no Plan B for our national parks"—Rand Abbott

"Donald Trump is literally destroying America."—Bill Prady

This morning, separating aloe pups, spider plant sprawl,
sage undergrowth, dried in drought. There she
ran along, over stone circles laid for steps when wet.
Today, so dry.
At first, a quiver, then quicker, run, low, steady, mammal.
Golden, buff, fur— endangered one in quiet refuge, this garden
Kangaroo
rat, related to beaver, pocket gopher
running along, making room for me to thin, separate
her lodging space, cover, home—
more hers than mine, endemic.

Yesterday, in Ventura County, a male gray wolf appeared,
for first time in ninety-nine years, here.

Dazzled under luminosity
nitric acid photons airglow field
100 thousand million stars in the sky road milk corn mush acorn
take some home
California, come home,
somewhere beyond brutal lies beauty,
unrequited,

requite now, quiet now, requite kindness,
mutual aid, reciprocal abundance, beauty
as far as land is poppied, Chaparral roam, bladderpod stand
let this dream, breath plume, vascular thrum
strengthen
stone tongues speaking in night as they shift along,
Playa sailing stones, wanderlusting
night unbroken, spirit unbroken,
drawing their lines in the sand

Your palms know where to go.
What they imagine leads you.
Everything we muster moves us along,

like water mirroring itself remembers
where to flow, how to go there.
In the dream you follow, in the dream we

fly over all of this direness float vaquitas.

We move like smallest porpoises, undulate in air, like swimming
arms tight against our sides
California spread below us
manzanitas gleaming in sun
stars ahead in darkness await our time there.
For now, it is the offering we make.

Look at This Blue

Hidden Lake bluecurls *from Hidden Lake, San Jacintos, Riverside County*

on the shores of a single vernal pool, ephemeral

trampling by hikers, sightseekers endangers

each flower a hairy calyx with pointed sepals

tubular corona

fifty flowers might fit on a penny

a member of the mint family

delisting, seeds stored in seed bank

vulnerable

Will you take me as I am?

California

—Joni Mitchell

Do the work:

Amah Mutsun Land Trust
Restoring Indigenous knowledge and practices
to Popeloutchom ancestral homelands
https://www.amahmutsunlandtrust.org

The Native American Land Conservancy's mission is to acquire, preserve, and protect sacred lands in aboriginal territories of Southern California.
http://nativeamericanland.org

Indian Land Tenure Foundation
https://iltf.org

NICWA
https://www.nicwa.org/about-icwa

CASA
https://casaforchildren.org

IRC
https://www.rescue.org/united-states/los-angeles-ca

Border Angels
https://www.borderangels.org

Justice in Motion
http://justiceinmotion.org

Kids in Need of Defense
https://supportkind.org

RAICES
https://www.raicestexas.org

Center for Empowering Refugees
https://www.cerieastbay.org

Intertribal Friendship House
https://www.ifhurbanrez.org

Southern California Indian Center
https://www.ocindiancenter.org

Ready California
https://www.caloes.ca.gov/ICESite/Pages/National-Preparedness-Month.aspx

Californians for Pesticide Reform
https://www.pesticidereform.org

Deep Medicine Circle
http://www.deepmedicinecircle.org

Dr. Rupa Marya, One Earth
https://www.oneearth.org/contributor/dr-rupa-marya

Peninsula Open Space Trust
https://openspacetrust.org

Association of Ramaytush Ohlone (ARO)
https://www.ramaytush.org

Water Resource Center Archives
https://www.watereducation.org/california-environmental-organizations-involved-water-issues

Cultural Conservancy
https://www.nativeland.org

Women's Earth Alliance
https://womensearthalliance.org

Sogorea Té Land Trust
https://sogoreate-landtrust.org

mak-'amham/Café Ohlone
https://www.makamham.com

Seventh Generation Fund
https://7genfund.org

Sovereign Bodies Institute
https://www.sovereign-bodies.org

Chris Remington, "Indigenous Communities and Environmental Stewardship," CapRadio *California Native*
https://www.capradio.org/news/insight/2017/08/16/insight-081617b

Black Lives Matter Los Angeles
https://www.blmla.org

Immigrant Legal Resource Center
https://www.ilrc.org/who-we-are

California Farmworker Foundation
https://californiafarmworkers.org

California Asian Pacific Islander Legislative Caucus
https://apicaucus.legislature.ca.gov/community-resources

Asian Prisoner Support Committee
https://www.asianprisonersupport.com

Asian Pacific Environmental Network
https://apen4ej.org/who-is-apen

APIENC
https://apienc.org

California Partnership to End Domestic Violence
https://www.cpedv.org

Write Girl
https://www.writegirl.org

California Indian Studies & Scholars Association
http://www.californiaindianstudies.org

California Indian Law Association
https://www.calindianlaw.org

California Native Plant Society
https://www.cnps.org

Los Padres Forest Watch: Sespe Condor Sanctuary
https://lpfw.org/our-region/wildlife/california-condor

End Extinction San Diego
https://www.endextinctionsandiego.org

Afternotes:

California Governor Gavin Newsom addressed the state's homelessness crisis from the city of Sebastopol in Sonoma County on Monday, where he signed a $12 billion bill for homeless funding. . . . "Opportunity should not just be for some people."

—KTVU

COVID-19 State Data Tracking
https://covid19.ca.gov/state-dashboard/#todays-update

Current California State Budget
http://www.ebudget.ca.gov

California Homelessness Tracking Site
https://www.bcsh.ca.gov/hcfc/hdis.html

California Endangered Species
https://wildlife.ca.gov/Conservation/CESA

Works Cited

Page xiii: Gillis, Tanya Tagaq. 2016. "Retribution." Track 2 on *Retribution*. Six Shooter Records, compact disc.

Page 6: Le Guin, Ursula K. "Concerning Ishi." The Ursula K. Le Guin Literary Trust. Accessed June 1, 2021. http://www.ursulakleguinarchive.com/Note-Ishi.html.

Page 6: Native Languages of the Americas. "Yana Indian Language (Yahi)." Accessed June 1, 2021. http://www.native-languages.org/yana.

Page 7: Cosgrove, Jaclyn, Alejandra Reyes-Velarde, and Alene Tchekmedyian. "'It's all going to burn': Man accused of setting Holy fire was a well-known troublemaker, neighbors say." *Los Angeles Times*, August 13, 2018. https://www.latimes.com/local/lanow/la-me-holy-firxe-arson-suspect-20180812-story.html.

Page 10: Jones, Jack, and Eric Malnic. "2 New Ojai Fires Erupt; Arson Seen: Body of Third Victim Discovered in Baldwin Hills." *Los Angeles Times*, July 4, 1985. https://www.latimes.com/archives/la-xpm-1985-07-04-mn-9120-story.html.

Page 11: Palos Verdes/South Bay Audubon Society. "Blue Butterfly Project." Accessed June 1, 2021. https://pvsb-audubon.org/blue-butterfly-project.

Page 17: California Legislature. Senate. *Civil detention facilities: state investigation*. SB-622. California Legislature, 2019–2020 regular session. Introduced February 22, 2019.

Page 18: Pilkington, Ed, and Martin Pengelly. "'Let it be an arms race': Donald Trump appears to double down on nuclear expansion." *Guardian* (U.S. edition), December 24, 2016. https://www.theguardian.com/us-news/2016/dec/23/donald-trump-nuclear-weapons-arms-race.

Page 19: Badash, David. "Handcuffs, BB Guns Found in Home of 8 Year Old Boy Allegedly Tortured, Killed Because He Was Thought to Be Gay." New Civil Rights Movement. November 3, 2017. https://www.thenewcivilrightsmovement.com/2017/11/handcuffs_bb_guns_found_in_home_of_8_year_old_boy_tortured_killed_because_he_was_thought_to_be_gay.

Page 20: Pearce, Tim. "California's Largest Utility Could Face Murder Charges for Sparking Wildfires." *Daily Caller.* December 31, 2018. https://dailycaller.com/2018/12/31/pge-murder-manslaughter-california.

Page 20: Serna, Joseph, and Matt Hamilton. "PG&E Pleads Guilty to 84 Counts of Involuntary Manslaughter over Camp Fire." *Los Angeles Times*, March 23, 2020. https://www.latimes.com/california/story/2020-03-23/pge-pleads-guilty-to-84-counts-of-manslaughter-over-paradise-fire.

Page 33 (begins on): U.S. Fish & Wildlife Service. ECOS: Environmental Conservation Online System. Accessed June 1, 2021. https://ecos.fws.gov/ecp0/reports/ad-hoc-species-report?kingdom=V&kingdom=I&status=E&status=T&status=EmE&status=EmT&status=EXPE&status=EXPN&status=SAE&status=SAT&fcrithab=on&fstatus=on&fspecrule=on&finvpop=on&fgroup=on&header=Listed+Animals.

Page 44 (begins on): State of California Natural Resources Agency. *State and Federally Listed Endangered, Threatened, and Rare Plants of California.* April 2021. https://nrm.dfg.ca.gov/FileHandler.ashx?DocumentID=109390.

Pages 54–55: Amah Mutsun Tribal Band. "History." Accessed June 1, 2021. http://amahmutsun.org/history.

Page 56: Lindsay, Brendan C. *Murder State: California's Native American Genocide, 1846–1873.* Lincoln: University of Nebraska Press, 2012.

Page 56: Bell, Horace. *Reminiscences of a Ranger, Or, Early Times in Southern California.* Los Angeles: Yarnell, Caystile & Mathes, Printers, 1881.

Page 56: Wallace, William A., ed. "Indian Arrests." *Los Angeles Star,* December 3, 1853. USC Digital Library. http://digitallibrary.usc.edu/digital/collection/p15799coll68/id/1610.

Page 56: See also Meares, Hadley. "Genocide, Slavery, and L.A.'s Role in the Decimation of Native Californians." KCET. June 29, 2016. https://www.kcet.org/shows/lost-la/genocide-slavery-and-l-a-s-role-in-the-decimation-of-native-californians.

Page 57: Blakemore, Erin. "The Enslaved Native Americans Who Made the Gold Rush Possible." History. A&E Television Networks. Updated August 31, 2018. https://www.history.com/news/the-enslaved-native-americans-who-made-the-gold-rush-possible.

Pages 57–58: Reséndez, Andrés. *The Other Slavery: The Uncovered Story of Indian Enslavement in America.* Boston: Houghton Mifflin Harcourt, 2016.

Page 58: Blakemore, Erin. "California's Little-Known Genocide." History. A&E Television Networks. Updated December 4, 2020. https://www.history.com/news/californias-little-known-genocide.

Page 63: Judicial Branch of California. "California Tribal Communities." California Courts. Updated 2021. https://www.courts.ca.gov/3066.htm.

Pages 63, 70: The Judicial Branch of California. "Jurisdiction in Indian Country." California Courts. Updated 2021. https://www.courts.ca.gov/8710.htm.

Pages 64–66: Hodge, Frederick Webb, ed. *Handbook of American Indians North of Mexico: Part I.* Smithsonian Institution, Bureau of American Ethnology. Washington, DC: Government Printing Office, 1907. https://digitalcommons.csumb.edu/cgi/viewcontent.cgi?article=1003&context=hornbeck_ind_3.

Pages 64–66: Wolf, Dan. "Chumash Tribe – Notes." *Keeper of Stories* (blog). February 27, 2012. http://keeperofstories.blogspot.com/2012/02/.

Pages 66–71: Magliari, Michael. "An American Genocide: The United States and the California Indian Catastrophe, 1846-1873." *Ethnohistory* 62, no. 2 (April 1, 2017): 341–342. https://doi.org/10.1215/00141801-3789465.

Pages 66–71: Akins, Damon, and William J. Bauer. *We Are the Land: A History of Native California.* Berkeley: University of California Press, 2021.

Pages 66–71: Wolf, Jessica. "Revealing the History of Genocide against California's Native Americans." Newsroom. UCLA. August 15, 2017. https://newsroom.ucla.edu/stories/revealing-the-history-of-genocide-against-californias-native-americans.

Pages 67–69: "California Genocide." Wikipedia. Updated May 25, 2021. https://en.wikipedia.org/wiki/California_genocide.

Pages 67–69: Madley, Benjamin. *An American Genocide: The United States and the California Indian Catastrophe*, 1846-1873. New Haven, CT: Yale University Press, 2017.

Pages 67–70: Glauner, Lindsay. "The Need for Accountability and Reparations: 1830-1976 the United States Government's Role in the Promotion, Implementation, and Execution of the Crime of Genocide against Native Americans." *DuPaul Law Review* 51, no. 3 (Spring 2002): 911–962. https://via.library.depaul.edu/cgi/viewcontent.cgi?article=1568&context=law-review.

Page 69: Susman, Amelia. "The Round Valley Indians of California: An Unpublished Chapter in *Acculturation in Seven (or Eight) American Indian Tribes.*" *Contributions of the University of California Archaeological Research Facility*, 31 (1976)." https://digitalassets.lib.berkeley.edu/anthpubs/ucb/proof/pdfs/arf031-004.pdf.

Page 70: Dobuzinskis, Alex. "California Governor Apologizes to Native Americans, Cites 'Genocide'." Reuters. June 18, 2019. https://www.reuters.com/article/us-california-native-americans/california-governor-apologizes-to-native-americans-cites-genocide-idUSKCN1TK03P.

Page 70: California Legislature. Senate. *An act to add Division 6.5 (commencing with Section 8575) to the Public Resources Code, relating to the Gabrielino-Tongva Tribe.* SB-1134. January 31, 2008.

Page 70: Blakemore, Erin. "California Slaughtered 16,000 Native Americans. The State Finally Apologized for the Genocide." History. A&E Television Networks. June 19, 2019. https://www.history.com/news/native-american-genocide-california-apology.

Page 71: Chamings, Andrew. "The Golden Dragon Massacre: A Bloody Rampage in 1970s SF." SFGATE, June 15, 2021. https://www.sfgate.com/sfhistory/article/golden-dragon-massacre-san-francisco-1977-16246542.php.

Page 71: Wallace, Kelly. "Forgotten Los Angeles History: The Chinese Massacre of 1871." Los Angeles Public Library. May 19, 2017. https://www.lapl.org/collections-resources/blogs/lapl/chinese-massacre-1871.

Page 71: Kesslen, Ben. "Gunman in 2018 Thousand Oaks Shooting Motivated by Hatred of College Students, Report Says." NBC News. July 1, 2021. https://www.nbcnews.com/news/us-news/gunman-2018-thousand-oaks-shooting-motivated-hatred-college-students-report-n1272936.

Page 71: Littlefield, Dana. "New Documentary Explores 1984 McDonald's Massacre in San Ysidro." *San Diego Union Tribune*, September 21, 2016. https://www.sandiegouniontribune.com/sd-me-mcdonalds-documentary-20160920-story.html.

Page 71: Johnson, Nikie. "San Bernardino Attack Timeline: Minutes of Terror, Years of Consequences." *San Bernardino Sun*, November 29, 2020. https://www.sbsun.com/2020/11/29/san-bernardino-attack-timeline-minutes-of-terror-years-of-consequences.

Page 71: Tsai, Joyce. "Memories on 50th Anniversary of Airplane Disaster in the East Bay Still Run Strong." *The Mercury News*, updated August 12, 2016. https://www.mercurynews.com/2014/05/06/memories-on-50th-anniversary-of-airplane-disaster-in-the-east-bay-still-run-strong.

Page 71: La Tour, Jesse. "The California Native American Genocide." *Fullerton Observer*, July 7, 2020. https://fullertonobserver.com/2020/07/07/the-california-native-american-genocide.

Page 73: Sacramento Fish & Wildlife Office. "Mission Blue Butterfly: Species Information." U.S. Fish & Wildlife Service. Updated December 1, 2017. https://www.fws.gov/sacramento/es_species/Accounts/Invertebrates/mission_blue_butterfly.

Page 74: McPhate, Mike. "California's black slaves and the myth of free soil." *California Sun*, January 23, 2019. https://www.californiasun.co/stories/californias-black-slaves-and-the-myth-of-free-soil.

Page 74: Fri, Robert. "Yana People to Receive Ishi's Brain." SFGATE, updated February 1, 2012. https://www.sfgate.com/opinion/openforum/article/Yana-People-To-Receive-Ishi-s-Brain-2931781.php.

Page 74: Southern Border Communities Coalition. "Deaths by Border Patrol Since 2010." Updated June 3, 2021. https://www.southernborder.org/deaths_by_border_patrol.

Pages 76–77: Ninan, Reena. "California Woman Valeria Alvarado Fatally Shot by Border Patrol Agent." ABC News. September 30, 2012. https://abcnews.go.com/US/valeria-alvarado-california-woman-fatally-shot-border-patrol/story?id=17359380.

Pages 76–77: U.S. Immigration and Customs Enforcement (ICE). "Detainee Death Report: SINGH, Simratpal." American Immigration Lawyers Association. Posted June 27, 2019. https://www.aila.org/File/Related/18121905f.pdf.

Pages 76–77: U.S. Immigration and Customs Enforcement (ICE). "Detainee Death Report: AMAR, Mergensana." American Immigration Lawyers Association. Posted June 27, 2019. https://www.aila.org/File/Related/18121905i.pdf.

Pages 76–77: U.S. Immigration and Customs Enforcement (ICE). "Detainee Death Report: RAMIREZ-ARREOLA, Augustina." American Immigration Lawyers Association. Accessed June 1, 2021. https://www.ice.gov/doclib/foia/reports/ddrRamirezArreolaAugustina.pdf

Pages 76–77, 82: U.S. Immigration and Customs Enforcement (ICE). "Detainee Death Report: TRAN, Huy Chi." American Immigration Lawyers Association. Posted December 19, 2018. https://www.aila.org/File/Related/18121905c.pdf.

Pages 76–77, 82: U.S. Immigration and Customs Enforcement (ICE). "Detainee Death Report: MIRIMANIAN, Gourgen." American Immigration Lawyers Association. Posted December 19, 2018. https://www.aila.org/File/Related/18121905.pdf.

Page 79: Adan, Melissa. "Family of Man Killed by Border Patrol Agent Says Non-Lethal Force Could've Saved His Life." CBS San Diego. Updated October 28, 2020. https://www.nbcsandiego.com/news/local/family-of-man-killed-by-border-patrol-agent-says-non-lethal-force-couldve-saved-his-life/2432195.

Page 82: McGreevy, Patrick. "California sues Trump over 'public charge' rule denying green cards to immigrants." *Los Angeles Times*, August 16, 2019. https://www.latimes.com/california/story/2019-08-16/california-immigration-lawsuit-trump-public-charge.

Page 85: Wiley, Hannah. "For 50th time, California sues the Trump administration — 'That's a lot of lawsuits.'" *Sacramento Bee*, May 13, 2019. https://www.sacbee.com/news/politics-government/capitol-alert/article230340579.html.

Page 85: Wolfe, Jan. "Trump sues California over tax return law." Reuters. August 6, 2019. https://www.reuters.com/article/us-usa-trump-california/trump-sues-california-over-tax-return-law-idUSKCN1UW22D.

Page 85: "Gov. Newsom Bashes Trump's Border Wall, Says California Won't 'Turn Its Back' On Asylum Seekers." CBS Los Angeles. March 11, 2019. https://losangeles.cbslocal.com/2019/03/11/newsom-interview-on-trump-border-wall.

Page 85: Stark, Kevin. "California sues Trump Administration over clean power rollback." KQED. August 13, 2019. https://www.kqed.org/science/1946454/california-sues-trump-administration-over-clean-power-rollback.

Pages 86–88: Garces, Audrey. "4 Bodies Recovered from Boat Fire off Santa Cruz Island." KQED. Updated September 2, 2019. https://www.kqed.org/news/11771713/boat-fire-off-southern-california-coast-leaves-34-missing.

Pages 86, 88: Anderson, Erik. "How Ice a Half a World Away Affects Southern California Sea Levels." KPBS Public Media. June 17, 2019. https://www.kpbs.org/news/2019/jun/17/how-ice-half-world-away-affects-southern-california.

Page 91: History.com editors, "This Day in History: Marvin Gaye Is Shot and Killed by His Own Father." History. A&E Television Networks. Updated March 30,2021. https://www.history.com/this-day-in-history/marvin-gaye-is-shot-and-killed-by-his-own-father.

Page 95: Colón-Muñiz, Anaida and Magaly Lavadenz, eds. *Latino Civil Rights in Education*. New York: Routledge, 2016.

Page 95: Rasmussen, Cecilia. "Institute Tried to Drum 'Civilization' Into Indian Youth." *Los Angeles Times*, February 23, 2003. https://www.latimes.com/archives/la-xpm-2003-feb-23-me-then23-story.html.

Page 95: Sherman Indian Museum. "Sherman Indian High School Beginning to the Present." Accessed June 1, 2021. http://www.shermanindianmuseum.org/sherman_hist.htm.

Page 95: Sherman Indian Museum. "Sherman Cemetery." Accessed June 1, 2021. http://www.shermanindianmuseum.org.

Page 96: Smith, Stacey. "Pacific Bound: California's 1852 Fugitive Slave Law." Black Past. January 6, 2014. https://www.blackpast.org/african-american-history/pacific-bound-california-s-1852-fugitive-slave-law.

Page 96: Library of Congress. "Primary Documents in American History: Chinese Exclusion Act." Accessed June 1, 2021. https://www.loc.gov/rr/program/bib//ourdocs/chinese.html.

Page 97: California Legislature. Senate. *An act to add Chapter 8.5 (commencing with Section 8720) to Division 1 of Title 2 of the Government Code, relating to Mexican repatriation.* SB-760, chapter 663. October 7, 2005.

Page 99: United States Congress. *Restitution for World War II Internment of Japanese-Americans and Aleuts.* U.S. Code 50, chapter 52, section 4201. August 10, 1988.

Page 115: Upton, John (@johnupton). "During the shutdown, with Joshua Tree National Park open but no staff on duty, visitors cut down Joshua trees so they could drive into sensitive areas where vehicles are banned." Twitter. January 10, 2019. https://twitter.com/johnupton/status/1083387896403505153.

Page 115: Chiu, Allyson. "A travesty to this nation': People are destroying Joshua trees in Joshua Tree National Park." *Washington Post*, January 11, 2019. https://www.washingtonpost.com/nation/2019/01/11/travesty-this-nation-people-are-destroying-joshua-trees-joshua-tree-national-park.

Page 115: Prady, Bill (@billprady). "They cut down Joshua trees. In Joshua Tree National Park. Donald Trump is literally destroying America." Twitter. January 10, 2019. https://twitter.com/billprady/status/1083441963515269120?lang=en.

Page 120: Mitchell, Joni. 1971. "California." Track 6 on *Blue*. Reprise Records, vinyl.

Index

126 Ventura Highway, 30, 102
Abbott, Rand, 115
Achulet (village), 67
Achulet Massacre, 67
Affordable Care Act, 85
Aleuts (Indigenous People), 99
Amah Mutsun Tribal Band (Indigenous People), 54, 55, 130
Amendment, Fifteenth, 74
Amendment, Fourteenth, 74
American Book Award, 98
Antarctica, 88
Asian and Pacific Islander Equality – Northern California (APIENC), 126
Asian Pacific Environmental Network, 126
Asian Prisoner Support Committee, 125
Association of Ramaytush Ohlone (ARO), 124
Baker, Milo, 50
Basins
  Los Angeles Basin, 70
  Santa Ana River Basin, 40
Becerra, Xavier, 85
Bell, Horace, 56
Betelgeuse (star), 42
Bidwell Ranch, 69
Big Sur fire, 31
Black Lives Matter Los Angeles, 125
Blood Alley. *See* 126 Ventura Highway
Bloody Island, 67
Bloody Island Massacre, 67
Bloody Rock, 67
Border Angels, 123
Bridge Gulch Massacre, 67
Brown, Jerry (former California governor), 70
Burnett, Peter Hardeman (first California governor), 58
Burpee Seed Company, 102
Calhoun, John C., 58
California
  Agoura Hills, 48
  Alameda, 41, 89
  Arcadia, 98
  Ash Meadows, 48, 49
  Ashland, 47
  Baja, 50, 94
  Bakersfield, 45, 50
  Big Sur, 31
  Butte County, 50
  Calistoga, 51
  Camp Seco, 67
  Carson, 36
  Chinese Camp, 46
  Colusa, 50
  Conejo, 48
  Contra Costa County, 48, 49
  Covelo, 69
  Cushenbury, 44, 45, 48
  Dehesa, 50
  Del Mar, 45
  Eastern California, 40
  El Dorado County, 49
  El Segundo, 33
  Encinitas, 45
  Fresno, 36, 98

Gaviota, 47
Humboldt County, 45, 69
Indian Country, 63, 70
Inland Empire, 34
Inyo, 40
  Fish Slough Ecological Reserve, 45
Kern County, 38, 48
Keyesville, 67
Kneeland, 50
La Graciosa, 47
Laguna Beach, 48
Lake County, 49, 51
Little Sur, 45
Livermore, 47
Lodi, 3
Lompoc, 48
Los Angeles, 56, 85, 91
  Baldwin Hills, 10
  Northridge, 29
Marin County, 49, 73
Mariposa County, 46, 50, 67
Merced, 47, 98
Mono County, 43
Monterey, 47, 52
Morro Bay, 36, 45
Napa, 51
North Coast, 40, 51
Oak Run, 67, 69
Oakland, 60, 89
Palos Verdes Peninsula, 11, 33
Pasadena, 43
Pine Hill, 46, 49
Pinedale, 98
Pismo Beach, 47
Point Arena, 36
Point Conception, 33
Point Reyes, 45, 49, 53
Pomona, 98
Poway, 93
Punta Abreojos, 33
Riverside, 5, 34, 98, 119
  Bordwell Park, 5
  Eastside, 5
  Emerson Elementary, 5
  Hidden Lake, 52, 119
  Jurupa Avenue, 107
  Martin Luther King Road, 5
  San Jacinto Valley, 45
  Stratton Community Center, 5
Sacramento, 50, 53, 98
Salinas, 98
San Benito, 46
San Bernardino, 36, 51, 71
San Bruno, 33, 45, 98
San Clemente, 36, 40
San Diego, 34, 44, 48, 61, 94, 126
San Fernando, 93
San Francisco, 1, 36, 39, 45, 49, 51, 6, 73, 98
  Bay Delta, 39
  Hyde Street, 59
  Mission District, 73
  Museum of Modern Art, 98
  Presidio Park, 45, 47
  State University, 59
  Turk Street, 59
San Joaquin, 34, 50, 51
San Mateo, 44, 48
San Pedro, 11
San Ysidro, 71
Santa Barbara, 36, 65
Santa Cruz, 34, 48, 49, 54
Santa Monica, 48

Santa Paula, 8, 102, 106, 111, 112
Glen City Elementary, 112
Harvard Boulevard, 106
Santa Susana, 47
Santa Ynez, 52, 102
Scotts Valley, 47, 51
Sebastopol, 50, 126
Shasta, 34, 67
Shingletown, 67
Siskiyou County, 46
Solano County, 52
Sonoma County, 36, 42, 44, 45, 47, 128
Southern California, 36, 42, 95, 126
Springville, 47
Stockton, 98
Suisun, 47
Tecopa, 42
Temecula, 67
Thousand Oaks, 71
Tiburon, 46, 52
Tipton, 36
Trinity County, 48
Truckee, 50
Tulare County, 42, 98
Ramshaw Meadows, 44
Turlock, 98
Twin Peaks, 73
Vallejo, 104
Ventura County, 13, 27, 30, 45, 65, 102
Fillmore, 30
Oxnard, 30
Piru, 30
Rancho Sespe, 30
Santa Paula, 30
Saticoy, 30
Vine Hill, 47
Woodland, 98
Yolo County, 70
Yreka, 51
Zayante, 33, 36
California Asian Pacific Islander Legislative Caucus, 125
California Farmworker Foundation, 125
California Genocide, 71
California Indian Law Association, 126
California Indian Studies & Scholars, 126
California legislature, 57, 96, 97
California Native Plant Society, 126
California Partnership to End Domestic Violence, 126
Californians for Pesticide Reform, 124
Camp Seco Massacre, 67
Canada, 38
Canyons
Camatta, 46
Cuesta Pass, 51
Metcalf, 52
Red Rock, 47
CapRadio *California Native* (serial), 125
Care Not Cash (government program), 60
Center for Empowering Refugees, 124
Central California Coast, 40
Channel Islands, 51, 86
Catalina, 46
San Clemente, 44, 46, 47, 49, 50

San Miguel, 34, 64
San Nicolas, 48
Santa Barbara, 48
Santa Catalina, 34
Santa Cruz, 34, 44, 48, 50, 52, 53, 64
Santa Rosa, 34, 45, 64, 66
Channel Islands Labor Day cruise, 86
Chico Creek, 67, 69
Chico Creek Massacre, 67
Chinese Exclusion Act of 1882, 96
Chinese Massacre, 71
Chumash (Indigenous People), 66, 102
Chumashan family, 66
Citizen 13660, 98
Civil Liberties Act of 1988, 99
Colorado, 36
Commissioner of Indian Affairs, 95
Constantinople, 56
Court Appointed Special Advocates (CASA), 123
COVID-19, 70, 71, 76, 80, 89, 127
Crowley, Father John, 50
Cultural Conservancy, 124
Customs and Border Protection, United States (CBP), 74
Dahlum, Timothy, 11
Daily Caller (news and opinion website), 20
Deep Medicine Circle, 124
Defense Fuel Support Point (San Pedro, California), 11
Department of Justice, United States, 17
Deserts
Colorado, 115
Mojave, 40, 47, 115
Sonoran, 33, 40
District of Columbia. *See* Washington, DC.
Dolan fire, 31
Dunes
Algodones, 49
Antioch, 50
Delhi, 34
Eureka, 50
Eel River Rangers, 69
El Niño, 88
End Extinction San Diego, 126
Executive Order 9066, 98
Flores y Cantos, 30
Florida, 57
Gilroy Garlic Festival, 93
Golden Dragon Massacre, 71
Grape Escape (boat), 87
Greenland, 88
Griffith Park Detention Camp, 98
Guadalupe, 39
Hoover, Robert Francis (botanist), 48
Howonquet Massacre, 67
Howonquet village, 67
Immigrant Legal Resource Center, 125
Immigration and Customs Enforcement, United States (ICE), 74
Immigration and Naturalization Service, United States (INS), 17
Indian Act of 1850, 57
Indian Flower Day, 95
Indian Island. *See* Tuluwat Island
Indian Island Massacre, 67, 69
Indian Land Tenure Foundation, 123

Internal Revenue Service, United States (IRS), 17
International Rescue Committee (IRC), 123
Intertribal Friendship House, 60, 124
Ishi, 6, 74
Jarboe, Walter, 67, 69
Jarboe's War Massacre, 67, 79
Joshua Tree National Park, 115
Justice in Motion, 123
KCET (news organization), 56
Kenwood Marsh, 52
Kern and Sutter Massacres, 67
Kern, Edward M., 67
Keyesville Massacre, 67
Kids in Need of Defense, 123
Kingsley Cave Massacre, 67
Klamath Lake Massacre, 67
Klamath River Massacres, 67
Konkow Maidu (Indigenous People), 67, 69
Konkow Maidu Slaver Massacre, 67
Konkow Trail of Tears Massacre, 67, 69
KQED (news organization), 85
KTVU (news organization), 126
Lahontan Reservoir, 40
Lakes
  Boggs, 49
  Buena Vista, 36
  Clear, 42
  Cuyamaca, 47
  Hidden, 52, 119
  Klamath, 67
  Lomond, 47
  Mono, 43
  Owens, 67
  Tahoe, 51
  Vail, 46
Le Guin, Ursula K., 6
Limoneira (agribusiness), 30, 102
Loma Prieta earthquake, 92
Los Angeles Star (newspaper), 56
Los Angeles Times (newspaper), 20, 82
Los Padres Forest Watch Sespe Condor Sanctuary, 126
Los Padres National Forest, 8
Lucha, La, 30
mak-'amham/Café Ohlone, 125
Manzanar Detention Camp, 98
Mariposa War Massacre, 67
Massacre at Bloody Rock, 67
Mattoni, Rudi, 11
Medicaid, 82
Mesas
  Nipomo, 50
  Otay, 47, 51
  San Diego, 51
Mexican Repatriation Program, 97
Mexico, 17, 49, 63
  Guanajuato City, 102
  Monterrey, 94
Miné Okubo, Nisei, 98
Missions
  Purísima, 65
  San Buenaventura, 65
  San Juan Bautista, 54, 55
  San Miguel Island, 64
  Santa Barbara, 65
  Santa Cruz Island, 54, 64
  Santa Inez, 64
  Santa Rosa Island, 64
Mitchell, Joni, 120

Mountains
Ben Lomond, 47
Irish Hills, 48
Laguna Mountains, 36
Mount Laguna, 47
Lassics, the, 50
Mount Diablo, 47
Mount Gleason, 46
Otay Mountain, 81
Red Hills, 52
Red Mountain, 52
San Bernardino Mountains, 51
Lane Mountain, 45
San Bruno Mountain, 73
San Jacinto Mountains, 119
Tahquitz Peak, 49
Santa Cruz Mountains
Butano Ridge, 49
Loma Prieta, 92
Mount Hermon, 33
Santa Lucia Mountains, 46, 51
Sierra Nevada, 35, 36
Topatopa Mountains, 28, 12
Mupu (Chumash village), 102
MV *Conception* (dive boat), 86, 87
National Indian Child Welfare Association (NICWA), 123
Native American Land Conservancy, 123
Native Studies, 60
New Orleans, Louisiana, 56
Newsom, Gavin, 70, 85, 126
Oak Run Massacre, 67, 69
Ohlone (Indigenous People), 37, 59, 62, 124, 125
Old Shasta Town Massacre, 67
Olivelands School, 30
One Earth, 124
Orcutt, Charles Russell, 46
Oregon, 38, 39
Sodaville, 45
Orion (constellation), 3
Owens Lake Massacre, 67
Ox Incident Massacre, 67
Pacific (geographic region), 36, 39, 45, 52
Pacific Air Lines, 71
Pacific Gas & Electric Company (PG&E), 20, 93
Panama Canal, 57
Parish, Samuel Bonsall (botanist), 48, 49, 51
Pauma Massacre, 67
Pendleton Wool Mills (company), 16
Peninsula Open Space Trust, 124
Perris Indian School, 95
Petty, Tom, 60
Phoenix (condor), 31
Piggly Wiggly (grocery store), 61
Pit River Massacre, 67
Pitkin Marsh, 46, 49
Pleiades (constellation), 80
Popeloutchom, 54, *See also* Amah Mutsun Tribal Band (Indigenous People)
Poway synagogue, 93
Prady, Bill, 115
Pribilof Islands, 99
Racetrack Playa (dry lake), 117
Ramaytush (Indigenous People). *See* Ohlone (Indigenous People)
Rancheria Tulea (Indigenous People), 67

Ready California, 124
Redwood Queen (condor), 31
Refugee and Immigrant Center for Education and Legal Services (RAICES), 123
Retribution (Tanya Tagaq album), xiii
Reuters (news organization), 85
Rivers
  Amargosa, 37, 50
  Chorro Creek, 47
  Cosumnes, 3
  Kaweah, 46
  Klamath, 67
  Little Kern, 40, 42
  Lost, 36
  Mojave, 37
  Pit, 67
  Sacramento, 57, 67
  Santa Ana, 48
Rogers, Rick, 11
Round Valley Reservation, 69
Round Valley Settler Massacre, 67, 69
Rust, Horatio N., 95
Sacramento Bee (newspaper), 85
Sacramento River Massacre, 67
San Ysidro McDonald's massacre, 71
Santa Ana winds, 28, 114
Santa Anita Racetrack, 98
Santa Paula Bank, 106
SB1134, 70
SB622 Civil Detention Facilities: State Investigation, 17
Scadden Flat, 52
Sequoia National Park, 42
Serra, Father Junípero, 55, 64
Seven Oaks Dam, 40
Seventh Generation Fund, 125
Sherman Indian High School, 95
Sherman Institute. *See* Sherman Indian High School
Shingletown Massacre, 67
Sogorea Té Land Trust, 125
Southern California Indian Center, 124
Sovereign Bodies Institute, 125
St. Vincent Medical Center (Los Angeles), 59, 60
State of California (governing body), 70, 96, 97, 98
Subaru (constellation). *See* Pleiades (constellation)
Subway (restaurant), 109
Supreme Court, California, 97
Sutter Buttes, 67
Sutter Buttes Massacre, 67
Sutter, John, 67
Sutter's Gold Rush, 57
Tagaq, Tanya, xiii
Tanforan Detention Camp, 98
Tanforan Racetrack, 98
Tapís, Father Estévan, 64
Temecula Massacre, 67
Three Knolls Massacre, 67
Tongva (Indigenous People), 70
Trail of Tears, 67
Travelers Aid, 59
Trump, Donald, 82, 85, 115
Tule Lake Detention Camp, 98
Tuluwat Island, 67, 69
Twisselmann, Ernest (botanist), 48, 50
Twitter, 18

University of California, Berkeley, 6, 98
Valleys
Big Bear, 48
Central, 38
Coachella, 38, 45
Indian, 46
Long, 45
Owens, 51, 98
Pauma, 67
Round, 67, 79
Sacramento, 42, 79
San Fernando, 46
San Jacinto, 45
San Joaquin, 50
Santa Clara, 47
Villalobos, Brittany, 79
Villalobos, David, 79
Vista Cove Care Center, 111
Vista del Mar, 103
Vizenor, Gerald, 68
Washington, DC, 85
Water Resource Center Archives, 124
West Coast (United States), 94, 98, 102
Wiyot (Indigenous People), 69
Women's Earth Alliance, 125
World War II, 99
Wright Massacre, 67
Wright, Ben, 67
Write Girl, 126
Xerces blue butterfly, 1, 43
Yahi. *See* Yana (Indigenous People)
Yana (Indigenous People), 6, 69, 74
Yana (language), 6
Yelamu (Indigenous People). *See* Ohlone (Indigenous People)
Yontocket Massacre, 67
Yontocket village, 67
Yosemite, 40, 44
Yuki (Indigenous People), 69
Yuma, Arizona, 36
Zayante Sand Hills, 33

Coffee House Press began as a small letterpress operation in 1972 and has grown into an internationally renowned nonprofit publisher of literary fiction, essay, poetry, and other work that doesn't fit neatly into genre categories.

Coffee House is both a publisher and an arts organization. Through our *Books in Action* program and publications, we've become interdisciplinary collaborators and incubators for new work and audience experiences. Our vision for the future is one where a publisher is a catalyst and connector.

LITERATURE
is not the same thing as
PUBLISHING

Funder Acknowledgments

Coffee House Press is an internationally renowned independent book publisher and arts nonprofit based in Minneapolis, MN; through its literary publications and *Books in Action* program, Coffee House acts as a catalyst and connector—between authors and readers, ideas and resources, creativity and community, inspiration and action.

Coffee House Press books are made possible through the generous support of grants and donations from corporations, state and federal grant programs, family foundations, and the many individuals who believe in the transformational power of literature. This activity is made possible by the voters of Minnesota through a Minnesota State Arts Board Operating Support grant, thanks to the legislative appropriation from the Arts and Cultural Heritage Fund. Coffee House also receives major operating support from the Amazon Literary Partnership, Jerome Foundation, McKnight Foundation, Target Foundation, and the National Endowment for the Arts (NEA). To find out more about how NEA grants impact individuals and communities, visit www.arts.gov.

Coffee House Press receives additional support from Bookmobile; Dorsey & Whitney LLP; Elmer L. & Eleanor J. Andersen Foundation; Fredrikson & Byron, P.A.; the Matching Grant Program Fund of the Minneapolis Foundation; Mr. Pancks' Fund in memory of Graham Kimpton; the Schwab Charitable Fund; and the U.S. Bank Foundation.

The Publisher's Circle of Coffee House Press

Publisher's Circle members make significant contributions to Coffee House Press's annual giving campaign. Understanding that a strong financial base is necessary for the press to meet the challenges and opportunities that arise each year, this group plays a crucial part in the success of Coffee House's mission.

Recent Publisher's Circle members include many anonymous donors, Patricia A. Beithon, Anitra Budd, Andrew Brantingham, Dave & Kelli Cloutier, Mary Ebert & Paul Stembler, Jocelyn Hale & Glenn Miller, the Rehael Fund-Roger Hale/Nor Hall of the Minneapolis Foundation, Randy Hartten & Ron Lotz, Dylan Hicks & Nina Hale, William Hardacker, Kenneth & Susan Kahn, Stephen & Isabel Keating, the Kenneth Koch Literary Estate, Cinda Kornblum, Jennifer Kwon Dobbs & Stefan Liess, the Lambert Family Foundation, the Lenfestey Family Foundation, Sarah Lutman & Rob Rudolph, the Carol & Aaron Mack Charitable Fund of the Minneapolis Foundation, Gillian McCain, Malcolm S. McDermid & Katie Windle, Mary & Malcolm McDermid, Daniel N. Smith III & Maureen Millea Smith, Peter Nelson & Jennifer Swenson, Enrique & Jennifer Olivarez, Alan Polsky, Robin Preble, Jeffrey Sugerman & Sarah Schultz, Nan G. Swid, Grant Wood, and Margaret Wurtele.

For more information about the Publisher's Circle and other ways to support Coffee House Press books, authors, and activities, please visit www.coffeehousepress.org/pages/donate or contact us at info@coffeehousepress.org.

Allison Adelle Hedge Coke, a California Arts Council Legacy Artist, Fulbright scholar, First Jade Nurtured SiHui Female International Poetry Award recipient, recent Dan and Maggie Inouye Distinguished Chair in Democratic Ideals, and U.S. Library of Congress Witter Bynner fellow, has written seven books of poetry, one book of non-fiction, and a play. Following former fieldworker retraining in Santa Paula and Ventura in the mid-1980s, she began teaching, and she is now a distinguished professor of creative writing at the University of California, Riverside.

Look at This Blue was designed by
Bookmobile Design & Digital Publisher Services.
Text is set in Lora Regular.